PHIL'S JAVA TUTORIAL
Java for the Autodidact

PHIL'S JAVA TUTORIAL
Java for the Autodidact

By

Philip Perry

Copyright 2007 by Philip Perry -- ALL RIGHTS RESERVED.

ISBN: 978-1-304-32766-6

This book is a copyrighted work, and I reserve all rights in accordance with the copyright laws of the United States of America. My copyright has been registered with the U.S. Copyright Office; this work was initially published in 2007.

Please note that I understand and respect "fair use" rights, and I won't make any effort to stop you from engaging in activities that fall within "fair use" under the laws of the U.S.A. (Even if your own country doesn't offer such protections).

Note also that there is a special PDF-only version of this Java tutorial available on my website. You may download this free PDF and use it according to a fairly liberal license grant you'll find on its copyright page.

YOU CAN FIND THE FREE PDF HERE:

http://www.tech-hermitage.com/JavaTutorial/

This book is dedicated to my parents, who patiently helped me get through college, the wandering phase I went through in my twenties, and the dot-com crash.
I miss them more than anything:

Janet Perry: 1935 - 2009

Philip Perry: 1936 - 2010

TABLE OF CONTENTS:

Chapter:	Title:	Page #:
	Preface	i
0	Some Useful Info	1
1	Preliminary Concepts	5
2	Java Variables and Data Types	13
3	Syntax, Conditional Statements, Looping, and Methods	31
4	Classes, Objects, and Interfaces (OOP)	49
5	Exception Handling	63
6	Working With the Filesystem	71
7	Using JDBC to Interact With Databases	79
8	Collections (ArrayList and HashMap)	97
9	Threads	105
10	A Very Short Chapter on Date and Time Manipulation	109
	Afterword	113

Preface

When I decided to re-learn Java in 2005 after a four year hiatus, most of the books I found in the store were huge boat anchors, 700 - 1200 pages long. Even the small ones were over 200 pages, with whole chapters on subjects like AWT and Swing despite the fact that modern development environments do much of that work *for* you. I was turned off by all this. I bought one of the smaller books, used only about 3/4 of it, and did the rest of my studying online, using forums, wikis, and tutorials.

This experience made me think that there's room in the world for a good, small book on Java. Such a book would tell the reader what he needed to know without boring him to death with nonsense filler. It would be under 150 pages, and it would concentrate on the parts of Java people actually have to work with to write real code. Most important of all, it would comfortably fit in a new programmer's courier bag, ready to be drawn out anytime he wanted to refresh his memory about the basics. Finally, the book would be available in a downloadable electronic form that the reader could put on a laptop or PDA. One problem I've noticed with online tutorials is that they're usually in HTML format, and aren't always available when you're behind an overzealous content-management system.

I spent a few months turning my idea into a real, physical book (you're reading it right now). I'm releasing it in two formats: a paper book that I'll sell online, and a PDF that I'll give away for free on my website. I'm granting a couple of extra permissions for readers of the PDF version so they can get the most use out of it; see the copyright page for more information.

Most readers will probably just download the PDF; I'm ok with that. But if you want a nice, professionally printed copy you can carry around with you, please consider buying one from me (they're only twenty bucks). The purchase price will help me pay for my website bandwidth and costs, and you'll get some good karma in return.

You can buy this book by browsing my website and blog, which you can find at http://tech-hermitage.com. I'll link to any on-demand publishers offering my book there. This way, you'll always see the current set of companies offering my work.

Oh, by the way -- thanks for reading my book. If you see any errors, mistakes, or anything you just want to chat about, feel free to email me at philipperry@tech-hermitage.com, or my alternate, Philip.TheHermit@gmail.com.

Philip Perry
December, 2007
Updated August, 2013

Most Recent Update:

August 14, 2013 (Reformatted book for 8 1/2 x 11 printing, updated the database chapter to direct readers to Apache Derby instead of the old Sun JavaDB project, corrected some NetBeans instructions, and updated broken links).

Chapter 0: Some Useful Info

A general philosophy for learning and using Java:

The most efficient way to learn any programming language is to learn the basics, get a feel for the language itself, and then pursue advanced topics separately (usually online).

It's a good idea to start trying to build simple projects as soon as possible. It familiarizes you with the Integrated Development Environment (IDE) you'll be using as well as the language itself. Try and work on mini-projects that force you to search the web for solutions, so you'll get practice learning new tricks and incorporating them into your repertoire. Get used to constantly researching anything new or different that comes up.

As you learn each new thing, write a small paper about it in a laboratory notebook, keeping notes about any problems you run into or solve. Once you're completely satisfied with each writeup, type it into your computer as a text file and store it with your other notes in some way you find easy to work with. Sooner or later, you'll want to review them (when a problem arises again, or someone asks you about an old solution you found) and these files will come in handy. A good approach is to store your notes in a set of directories on your computer, with one directory for each topic (don't just dump your notes in one huge directory; the clutter will make it hard to use). You'll also want to print out copies for offline reading; you can staple them together like a book using a large capacity stapler (available in office supply stores for around 40 bucks). If you do this, staple your notes along the left or top margin, not in the upper left hand corner (it makes them easier to read).

One final thing: Whenever you're trying to solve some new problem, before you do anything else, look for a solution in the Java libraries and online. Chances are someone else has already solved your problem and offers an open-source download that will help. It's always worth a look; you might not have to reinvent the wheel. For example, three years ago I needed to generate PDFs in some software I was writing. Instead of hacking together my own tool, I used Google and found the Lowagie iText package. My problem was solved in a week instead of months.

PRETASKS: Downloading and Installing the JDK and the Documentation:

If you're going to learn Java, the first thing you're going to need is a development environment. You'll need to download two pieces of software, the Java Development Kit (JDK) and a suitable Integrated Development Environment (IDE).

In my opinion, you should probably download the latest version of the Java Development Kit (JDK) that is distributed on Sun's Java site (unless you're running an Apple Macintosh, most of which come with a JDK already installed). You can download a JDK for free here:

http://java.sun.com/javase/downloads/index.jsp

If you're going to have some Apple Macintosh users, you should probably stick to JDK 1.5, because you won't be able to guarantee that your user's machines have any newer runtime environment (JRE) installed. Currently, since Apple still maintains their own internal version of Java, you're dependent on their release cycle, and on whether their users have upgraded their O/S. Users with modern machines will have a modern JDK; users with older machines will usually NOT. Your IDE should allow you to set the "code level" of your software to account for this issue.

Once you've got a JDK installed, you'll need an Integrated Development Environment (IDE). I use NetBeans, and I highly recommend it. It's free, it's got the best visual designer available, and it's easy to use. You can find it here:

http://www.netbeans.org

The next thing you're going to want to get is a local copy of Sun's amazingly good documentation, including *in particular* their API reference. You can find their documentation bundles, organized by Java version, here (make sure you pick up the correct version) :

http://java.sun.com/javase/reference/api.jsp

Click on the word "English" next to an appropriate Java version in "JDK Programmer Guides" to bring up the correct documentation in your browser, then click the "Download this documentation" link in the upper right hand corner to get your local copy. In the documentation, along the top, you can click "API, Language and VM specs" and then "Java Language API Specification" to get into the API reference itself. This is a three-frame setup where you can search top-notch documentation on every Java class in the standard library (which comes included with the JDK).

Once this is safely saved somewhere on your computer, keep it handy. The API reference is the Java programmer's BIBLE. Keep a copy open in a browser whenever you're programming, so you can look up classes and research different ways of accomplishing your tasks.

Once you've followed all the instructions and everything has been installed, you'll be able to start experimenting with Java. You'll want to start playing around with NetBeans first; get used to the IDE before you start trying out sample code. In practice, you'll want to do all your coding within NetBeans rather than on the command line. This is one of the ways in which I differ from most authors. I think you're at your most efficient within an IDE, and that tinkering around with Java in text mode is (almost) a complete waste of time. About the ONLY three useful command-line things you'll ever need to do will be:

A) get Java to give you a version number if you're not sure what you're running -- you can do this from any command shell with a "java -version". This also shows you whether you've got a JDK or JRE (Java Runtime Environment) installed.

B) in the event you write something in Java that is supposed to run in batch mode, you'll want to create a command line script that runs it so you can feed that to a scheduler. This is easy; you'll generate your Java program in NetBeans, export it to a JAR file, and run it with the command line "java -jar myProgram.jar".

C) When you create a "shortcut" that lets you fire off one of your Java programs, the actual command behind the shortcut will be the same "java -jar myProgram.jar" you use for batch mode, although in this case you won't be manually initiating it.

Anyway, clearly it's my opinion that you should do all of your development within NetBeans, and when you're ready to roll out your code, you should use the IDE's deployment tools to generate a JAR file (Java ARchive). Alternately, if you're developing for a website, you'll generate a WAR (Web ARchive) file. Let's spend a moment discussing these.

JAR files are incredibly convenient. They contain all your required libraries and can be double-clicked by your users as if they were regular desktop applications -- it's an ease of use miracle. When you want to roll a new version out, you can just bundle up another JAR for your users, clobbering the old one. If you wanted to create these from the command line, you'd be passing LOTS of parameters, but you can do it from NetBeans with a few mouseclicks.

WAR files work similarly, but you deploy them using a tool on your application server and let the server figure out how to set things up. Here, too, when you have a new version of your app, you can just roll it out with a few mouseclicks.

By the way, if you learn anything from me at all, learn this: it's ALWAYS a good idea to do things the easy way. Doing it the easy way means being more efficient, more productive, and ultimately, cheaper for your boss to support.

NOTE: On Choosing an IDE:

You won't get very far as a programmer without an Integrated Development Environment (IDE). There are a number of them available for Java, and although they're *similar* in most respects (i.e. they offer similar tools), they're not actually the same. In this brief aside, I'll tell you what I think of the IDEs I like to use, and hopefully point you in a practical direction.

I personally prefer Oracle's JDeveloper and Sun's NetBeans, because I like to write client-side applications software and each of these has an excellent User Interface (UI) designer built in. Furthermore, both are top-notch, have good debuggers, and make it relatively easy and painless to work with code and roll out your finished product to your users or a web server. Also, not that I'm cheap or anything, I love the fact that I can download either one for free. Free is good.

There ARE other IDEs out there, and you're welcome to check them out if you wish, but if you want my advice, you should choose one of these two. I personally lean towards NetBeans, and recommend it heartily to you.

Now for a Useful Tip:

Of course, while you learn you'll want to set up a sort of test rig, where you can type little snippets of code and see what they do. It's important to be able to do this; every Java programmer does it regularly. You might be calling a date function to see what its output looks like, or testing a random number feature you're playing with. Or maybe you want to see something O/S specific, like what happens when you output a special character like the one that triggers the system bell. Maybe you just want to fool around a little, and write something that produces ASCII art. Whatever. You need a quick way to run code and see its output. Let's take a minute and set up a small test program in NetBeans, so you'll be able to try out anything you want.

First, on the toolbar, around the upper left hand corner of the NetBeans window, you'll see a "New Project" icon. Let the mouse hover over the icons; the tooltip that comes up will tell you what the icon does. Clicking the icon starts the "new project" wizard. Now, under "Categories" choose Java, and under "Projects" choose "Java Application". Click "Next". Now, choose a name for your project, and click "Finish". Your test application will appear in the main NetBeans window.

Now, in the code for the application, look for "public static void main(String args[])". This method is the one that will be called when your program is run. It's basically the same as the main() method in a C program. Try out the following code for now, typing it in between the "{" and the "}" of main:

Sample Code Snippet to Try In NetBeans:

```java
try{
    System.out.println("Say it. \n\n");
    System.in.read();
    System.out.println("You said it. \n\n");
}
catch(Exception e){
    // Nothing to do here, just testing
}
```

Now, to see the code run, click the word "Run" up in the menu bar, then "Run Main Project". An output area will appear at the bottom of the screen, and you'll see some compiler output, then the word "run:" and then, your program's output. Click the output area to make it active, type something, and hit the enter key. You'll see "You said it" and a message that your build was successful.

The important things to note in this little bit of code are the methods you use to do output and input from a console. As I've said, you won't be doing much console programming as a Java programmer, but you can use the methods that apply to it to do input and output in the program output window in NetBeans. It's a neat little trick, and it'll let you try out sample code and test your thoughts as you read the rest of my little book.

Keep the try/catch block, and type your code in between the "{" and the "}" of the try block, where I've got my three i/o statements. It's quick and dirty, but sometimes, that's all you need, right?

Conventions I'll Follow In This Book:

Most of the book will use normal text, with headings in ***bold, underlined italic***.

Examples and syntax descriptions will have a shaded background. Code comments will be in *italics*. Syntax will be illustrated in **bold**. Examples will be in ordinary text. Headings for examples will be ***bold, underlined italic***. When I show you syntax, I'll put placeholders where you're supposed to substitute your own values in `**bold,underlined monospaced text**`.

One note about this new version of my tutorial: previously I had used Times New Roman and Courier, which are not normally available on Fedora systems because they are not "libre" fonts. I have decided to convert all the fonts in this book to libre fonts, specifically "Liberation Serif" for most text and "Liberation Mono" for monospaced text. These fonts are open-source, thus free for everyone to use as they see fit. I will also be saving my PDFs in "PDF/A-1a" format (used for long-term preservation of documents). This means my chosen fonts will be embedded in the document for worry-free viewing regardless of what fonts are available on a viewer's system.

Chapter 1: Preliminary Concepts

Many programmers are unfamiliar with Java syntax, which derives ultimately from C and Smalltalk. Many authors presume (incorrectly, I think) that programmers will have worked with this syntax in college, and their books seem to carry a built-in assumption that the basics are simple enough to pick up on the fly. The result is that many books are discouraging to programmers who have never worked with any of the C family of languages.

As a state government employee, I met people whose only experience was in writing JCL or COBOL on a creaky old mainframe. Some of these old-timers never studied C or anything like it, and for them, Java is utterly alien, a strange language that doesn't make any sense. They don't just need to learn the language's syntax; they need to learn a whole new set of abstractions and basic ideas. Everything in Java is different from what they're used to.

This chapter is my way of trying to make things a little easier for you if you're coming from a non-C, non-OO background. I'm going to provide you with an initial vocabulary of Java concepts so you'll be on less shaky ground as we move on to more interesting things. Of course, I'll go into a lot more detail in other chapters, but at least you'll have some idea up-front of what's going on. Also, if something isn't clear later, you'll be able to flip back to this chapter and refresh your memory.

If you've already worked with the C family of languages, you should still skim over this chapter. It may seem a little basic to you, but it'll be useful to review the material.

Let's start out by looking over an actual, working (if empty so far) piece of Java code. It won't mean anything to you right away, but look it over. Get a feel for how Java looks in general. Flip back to it as you read through the definitions. I've placed it on the next page to make it easier to read.

Example : A Working Java Program (that doesn't do anything yet):

```java
/*
 * This is a multi-line comment.
 * See how it lets you enter multiple lines?  Everything between the starting
 * slash-asterisk and the ending asterisk-slash is a comment.
 */

// This is a single-line comment.  Everything after the "//" is part of the comment.

package quicktests;        // The package THIS file belongs to.

import java.util.HashMap;  // This imports just the HashMap package.
import java.util.*;        // This imports all packages in Java.util.

// Here's the class declaration.
public class GenericTestProgram {

    // Here's the "constructor" method. This one doesn't
    // do anything. Note that it has exactly the same
    // name as the class.

    public GenericTestProgram() {
        // Nothing in the constructor yet.
    }

    // This is the "main" method. Java desktop applications
    // must provide a main method so the operating
    // system (and JVM) have an entry point into the
    // program. Its parameter is an array of strings
    // called args; these are command line arguments
    // you have set -- they're automatically passed in.
    // I'll tell you more about "main" when we get to
    // the chapter on "methods".

    public static void main(String[] args) {

        // Put any code you want to test in here.  I use this file to try code out, usually
        // when I'm trying out something weird to see if it'll work.

    }

}
```

Important Initial Definitions:

1. **Statements:** Each individual command or instruction you write in a Java program is called a "statement". Statements that involve loops or decisions can contain blocks of other statements, which we explain in #6, below. All statements end with semicolons (";") except statements that end with blocks (blocks are never followed by semicolons).

2. **Expressions:** An expression is not an entire statement by itself; rather, it is a chunk of code that when run, results in a specific value like "135" or "Philip". It can be as simple as a value like "test", or it can be a chunk of code that fetches a value back from a database. As long as it evaluates to a real, concrete value, it is an expression.

3. **Conditions:** Conditions are expressions that evaluate to a boolean "true" or "false" value. They're used in conditional statements to determine whether one or another action will take place.

4. **Code:** Your Java statements, taken together, are called your "code". When you write your Java program, you are "coding" it. Statements are also called "lines of code".

5. **Comments:** Throughout your code, you'll want to include comments, which won't affect your program but which will leave notes on what you're thinking, planning, and doing. Comments look like the example below. Use them liberally to keep track of why you're doing something and whether it has any special significance. Try not to comment about purely banal stuff like whether "i" is a counter; that should be obvious from your code.
Single-line comments contain two slashes ("//"); everything after the slashes is part of the comment. Multi-line comments start with a slash and an asterisk ("/*") and end with an asterisk and a slash ("*/"). Everything between the two symbols is part of the comment.

Example: Comments:

```
// This is a single-line comment. Almost all
// Java comments are single-line comments.
// Everything from the two slashes to the end of
// the line is part of the comment. You cannot put
// any more code on a single-line comment line.
/*
 * This is a multi-line comment.
 * It can hold multiple lines of text. Traditionally,
 * you should put an extra asterisk at the start of
 * each line to improve readability. .
 */
```

6. **Blocks:** Everything in Java is organized into blocks of code -- they begin and end with curly brackets. The following example demonstrates an "if" statement that contains a block of code (to simplify the example, I just put a comment in the block, but in "real life" you'd write some code there). In this case, the if, the condition (i < 10), and the two blocks are all considered to be parts of one big statement (a statement that contains two blocks of statements). Note that traditionally, Java programmers indent the contents of their blocks by four spaces (it's a good idea to set up your editor to insert four spaces when you hit "tab").

Example: If Statement With Block, K&R Style:

```
if(i < 10) {
    // pretend there's some code here
} else {
```

```
    // pretend there's some code here.
}
```

At this point, I think I should mention that there are two styles currently in use for the placement of curly brackets. The one I use is called "K&R", after the two inventors of the C programming language (Kernighan and Ritchie). In their book on C, they advocated a style that puts the opening bracket on the same line as the statement that begins the block, and the closing bracket on its own line, indented at the same level as the beginning statement.

The other style is called "BSD/Allman Style", named for Eric Allman, the creator of Sendmail. Some think his brace style is more readable. Here's an example of BSD/Allman style:

<u>*Example: If Statement With Block, BSD/Allman Style:*</u>
```
if(i < 10)
{
    // pretend there's some code here
}
else
{
    // pretend there's some code here
}
```

K&R style tends to be more compact, and produces tighter looking code that's easier to print out when you want to scan through it on paper with a highlighter and a marker. Allman style tends to be easier to scan through on your PC because the opening and closing brackets line up vertically.

If you use Sun's Netbeans IDE , you'll notice that the code it generates is K&R style. I believe this is the standard at Sun, because their own code samples are always K&R and the style guide Sun released advocates it as the standard approach. Further, the "Style Guide for Java Programmers" you'll see in bookstores (I recommend it, it's useful) recommends K&R.

On the other hand, if you use one of the other commercial IDEs, you're likely to see Allman style braces. For example, JDeveloper tends to use Allman style when it generates code. This probably represents the personal style of the team at Oracle that released it. Also, Apple's XCode seems to default to Allman style brackets.

Personally, I consider K&R to be "The One True Brace Style". My advice to you is this: If you work in an office where your boss has standardized on a specific style, use it. If you're free to use whatever style you like, go for K&R, which is what almost everyone else is using.

7. **Variable (also called "member", or "member variable"):** Variables are placeholders you declare that represent data in your program. There are two types of variables, corresponding to the two types of data in a Java program: primitives and reference variables. primitives simply hold a value, like the number 1 or the letter 'A'. Reference variables refer to objects in memory; in other words, they hold a memory address that points at some chunk of data. Simply enough, if a variable is declared to be a primitive type, it will be a primitive variable. If it's declared to be an object type, it will be a reference variable. I'll explain more in the next chapter, when we talk about data types.

8. **Method (also called "function"):** Methods are blocks of code that will be frequently used, and are "broken out" separately so they only have to be written once. Other programming languages call methods "procedures" or "functions" but the basic idea is the same. Methods will be explained in detail later on; for now, realize that they have a method name, a list of variables (called parameters) that you can pass to them, a return value (which can be "void", i.e. nothing) and a block of code that they execute when called. You can see two methods in the sample code earlier in the chapter.

9. **Class:** Almost all Java code is written as part of a class, within a single large block. Classes contain both variables and methods. Each class represents some discrete real-world thing. Its variables map to the real-world thing's characteristics; its methods map to things the real-world thing can do.

Take a class that models a real-world computer for example. Its members would include the make and model, the amount of RAM, the size of the hard disk, and so on. Its methods might include connecting to the Internet, sending email, and asking a user to log in. Everything that's particular to a computer would be contained within its class, or "**encapsulated**" within it.

Classes can be "**extended**" by other classes which are **derived** from them. Our computer class might be extended by a "laptop" class, which automatically "**inherits**" all of the members and methods of a computer class but adds some more related to portability. It might also be extended by a "server" class, which would add things only a server can do, like process web page requests. Here, we would say that our laptop and server classes "**extend**" our computer class. Also, in this example, the computer class would be considered the "**parent**" class, and the laptop and server classes would be thought of as "**child**" or "**derived**" classes.

10. **Object:** An object is a class that has been "**instantiated**" (created in your computer's memory by your program using your class as a blueprint). Every task in Java is handled by objects; there's almost nothing you can do without them. To initially instantiate a class, you simply assign it to a variable of the correct type using the "**new**" keyword (more on this a lot later, but here's an example).

Example: Instantiation of a "Person" object:

Person somebody = new Person();

11. **Constructor:** All classes have a constructor, which is a method (function defined within the class) named in exactly the same way as the class. The constructor is used for initial setup of the class. You can pass it **parameters** (variables you send the function when you call it), but this is optional. You can have multiple constructors with different sets of parameters if you wish. More on this in the "Classes and Objects" chapter. Whenever you use "new" to create a new object, the constructor is called automatically.

12. **Accessing class/object members and methods with 'dot' notation:** So far, you've learned that classes contain both members (data) and methods (functions) that can act on that data. Now I'm going to tell you how to actually access them. It's easy: you simply use the name of the object you're using, followed by a dot ("."), followed by the member or method you want to access. If your object is part of a package, you can list the whole chain of packages down to your object first, or you can "import" the package your class is in and just use the class name by itself. Consider this example, which uses a "Person" object:

Example: Accessing class/object members and methods using dot notation:

// Case 1: a "Person" class with member variable "message" and method
// "sendMessageToPerson":

Person somebody = new Person();
somebody.message = "Meeting at 10AM in A-4";
somebody.sendMessageToPerson();

// Note that for methods, even if you're not passing any
// parameters, you still have to include the parenthesis.

13. **Has a/Is a relationships:** Classes can have two possible relationships to other classes. If one class is a child of another, its relationship to its parent is an "is a" relationship because it "is a" derivative of the parent class. A laptop "is a" computer, for example. On the other hand, if a class contains another class as one of its members, it is said to have a "has a" relationship to it. If you were to create a "hard drive" class, then a laptop's relationship to the hard drive class would be "has a" because a laptop has a hard drive.

14. **Package:** A hierarchical set of classes that go together in some logical way and can be imported into your code as a unit. You'll use packages all the time in Java, especially when you **import** tools from the standard library (an import statement is just a way of saying that you intend to use a package in your code). Usually each package specializes in doing some specific type of task, for example, java.net relates to networks.

15. **Library:** Don't consider a "library" to literally be a different construct from a package. It's not, really. It's usually used in an informal sense to mean "a set of packages that someone has provided me with". The main library you're going to want to get used to is the standard library that comes with J2SE. It does just about everything and has a good API reference.

16. **public static void main(String[] args){ }** : If the program you are working on is a Java "application" (a regular program running on your desktop computer) one of your classes MUST have a "main" function and must be designated as your "main" class. When the Java Virtual Machine runs your program, it will start executing by calling the main function. In other words, main is the entry point to your program. Not all Java code works this way!

17. **Java Virtual Machine (JVM)** : Although languages like C or C++ are always compiled to machine code, a Java compiler compiles to "**bytecode,**" which is a sort of intermediate representation of your program. In the most basic case, that of a regular Java application running on a user's PC, the following sequence of events takes place:

    How a Java program is created, distributed, and used:

    A) You write your program and compile it to bytecode.

    B) You give your bytecode (usually as a JAR file, more on that later) to a user.

    C) The user runs your bytecode using a Java Virtual Machine he's installed on his PC. Most people have the official Sun "JRE" or Java Runtime Environment installed, but be aware that there are others offered by companies like IBM.

    D) The Java Virtual Machine reads your bytecode and uses a "Just In Time Compiler" to convert it to machine code before executing it, usually caching it for later (so it'll run much more quickly next time).

    E) The user enjoys your software.

    That's how it works in a general sense, anyway. If you understand the jist of it, you know enough to work with it.

    Although not all Java programs are Java applications, ALL Java programs are run in a virtual machine, without exception. The virtual machine basically acts as the middleman between the operating system and your Java program, so you don't have to worry about low-level system details. Of course, "no plan is perfect" so you'll still have to test your applications on every platform (Windows, Mac OS/X, Linux, FreeBSD, etc) you want to run them on. This is often humorously referred to as Java's "Write Once, Test Everywhere" approach, but it's a hell of a lot easier than working with an old-style compiled language (where you'd have to customize a "makefile" for each platform and compile over and over, THEN test).

18. **Garbage Collection**: Java, unlike languages like C and C++, manages memory allocation and deallocation FOR you using a system called "garbage collection". This feature is built into the JVM, and runs in the background looking for objects that no longer have any reference variables referring to them. Once an object is no longer referred to anywhere in your program, it is cleared out of memory and that memory is made available to your program again. Remember two important things about garbage collection as you work with Java. First, you cannot predict when the garbage collector will clean up an object, so try not to let your program use too much memory. Second, NEVER try to force garbage collection to run using gc() (as is suggested occasionally online). It'll slow down your program like nobody's business. Just let garbage collection do its thing and keep an eye on your memory use.

    (This will make more sense when we start talking about reference variables in the data types chapter).

19. **Strings:** Strings are objects that hold text, like "foo" or "123". Anything you would consider plain text (i.e. something you would be comfortable putting between double quotes) can be stored in a String. They are arguably the most important data type in Java, because without them you can't really do ANYTHING. We'll be talking about them in the next chapter. But since we have to mention them while talking about other data types, I wanted to mention them in advance so you'll know what we're talking about.

20. **Encapsulation:** In object oriented programming, when we talk about "encapsulation," we're saying that everything that relates to an object is contained within it. In other words, objects are totally self-

contained. Since an object is a representation of some real-world concept usually, this means that everything about that concept and everything that concept can do in your program should be contained within the object itself. This means the object isn't dependent on (i.e. "**tightly coupled**" to) anything outside of it.

When you design a class, you should think of it in terms of a singular thing, something that you could give another programmer to use as a tool. You should be able to hand it off to your coworkers with little more than a quick writeup on the public methods and members available to them. Your objects, then, should act as black boxes that are fed inputs, do something useful, and spit out useful outputs. Other programmers should never have to worry about what's inside of them.

Encapsulation is one of the three pillars of object oriented programming. The next two, inheritance and polymorphism, follow:

21. **Inheritance:** As you design your classes, you will be moving from a very general version of them towards more specific versions. As you build each more specific version, you don't have to cut and paste any code from your more general versions. You simply instruct the class to "extend" (inherit) the general version (as we discussed earlier). All YOU have to write is the part that will be different from the general version.

22. **Polymorphism:** A variable of a given class type can ALSO hold any object that was derived from that class type.

    Consider this example: you have a base class "car" which has a method "drive". You've created two child classes "automatic" and "stickShift". You can declare a "car" variable and instantiate it with either the "automatic" or "stickShift" child classes. Each of these has its own customized "drive" method. The automatic drive method just puts the car in "D" and goes. The stickShift drive method pushes the clutch, shifts into first, and goes.

    When you're using your "car" variable, you don't have to know whether you've got a clutch or an automatic or some other type of car. You just call the "drive" method and the Java Runtime Environment knows which version of the method to call. This is because the JRE knows which type of object you instantiated, even though you're using a top-level "car" variable to hold it. THAT is "Polymorphism".

23. **Access Modifiers:** While programming in Java, you'll want to exert some control over which parts of your classes other programmers can access. Your classes should usually be considered "black boxes" by those you share them with. In fact, the whole POINT of having classes is that once you build some functionality, it should work exactly the same way everywhere it's used, and if any changes need to be made, the only have to be made in one single place (the class itself).

    Java offers you several "access modifiers" so you can hide part of your functionality and enforce a consistent interface, thus guaranteeing that your code will work the way you intended it to. You apply these access modifiers to member variables and methods in order to force programmers to use your classes correctly.

    The modifiers you'll use most often are "public", "protected", and "private". Public means "everybody can access this member or method". Protected means "This class and all classes derived from it can access this member or method." Private means "Only THIS class can access this member or method." Usually I make my class members and methods protected, so I can work with them in child classes.

24. **Static members and methods:** Java offers a special keyword, "**static**", which allows you to tell the Java Runtime Environment that you want to make certain members and methods in your classes available even if an object of that type hasn't been instantiated yet. These members and methods will ALWAYS be available if the class they belong to has been imported into your code.

    For example, the class "Integer" has a "parseInt" method that is static. So, in your code, you can call "Integer.parseInt(someNumberString)" without having to instantiate an Integer object.

    You'll be using "static" often. In fact, every Java application has at least one static method in it: the "main" method that acts as the operating system's entry point to your code. The main function is static so the operating system can see it and run it even though technically no classes have been instantiated when your code is first run.

Be careful using static, though. When you make a member static, no matter how many objects you instantiate, they're all using the same exact member across the board because there's only one copy -- it no longer relates to or depends on a specific instance of the object. For this reason, you're better off only using static with constants and methods.

25. **Final:** In Java, when you mark a variable as "Final" you are making it a constant that cannot be changed. If you mark a variable "static final" it's a constant that's available even if you haven't instantiated the class it's contained in yet. If you mark a variable as Final you MUST give it a value right away because you won't be able to assign anything to it later. Methods can be final also, and when they are, they cannot be altered in a class' derived classes. Note that this is a little anti-social and should be avoided.

How Other Types of Java Programs Run:

As an aside, since we mentioned how regular Java programs are run by the JVM, we should briefly touch on the fact that not all java code runs that way. There are several types of Java code you can write, and each type runs differently.

If you're building a Java **servlet** (a dynamic, web accessible program that web pages can post forms to)**,** you won't have a main program at all. Instead, you'll have "doPost" and "doGet" functions that correspond to the POST and GET methods of the web page (and form) that accessed your servlet. These are executed by your web server automatically when the servlet is accessed. Think of a servlet as a sort of Java-oriented CGI program. In this case, your JVM was probably installed as part of a "servlet container" like Apache Tomcat. When a web page posts to it, your servlet will run automatically.

If you're building a **JSP** web page, your code is executed in order when the web page is loaded. This ALSO executes in a "servlet container". In fact, JSPs are compiled into servlets before they are executed. JSPs are nice; they work like regular web pages, but Java code contained within JSP tags runs on the server before the page is sent down to the browser. JSPs are usually used with a framework like Struts or JSF, and are generally used as a front-end.

Applets (Java programs you can embed in a web page) use a completely different mechanism. I won't get into that in this book; for a nice treatment of Swing applets, check out "Java for the World Wide Web (Visual Quickstart Guide)" by Dori Smith; it seems to contain a complete introduction to applet writing. I've got a copy or two floating around here, myself. If your local bookstore doesn't carry it, you can find it online at any of the big booksellers like Amazon.com. It's a nice, compact, easy to follow book.

Finally, JAVA IS NOT JAVASCRIPT!

I'll close the chapter out with an important piece of information: Java is not Javascript! A pet peeve of mine is that some people tend to confuse these two languages. Java is a full-power 3GL software development language like its forebears Smalltalk, C, and C++. You can do systems-level stuff in Java. Javascript, on the other hand, is a scripting language originally designed by Netscape Corporation in the mid-1990's. It was originally called "Mocha", then "LiveScript", and finally renamed "Javascript" to try and cash in on some of Java's popularity (at the time, Java was already in wide use). Javascript is properly called "ECMAScript" because it was adopted as an ECMA (European Computer Manufacturing Association) standard.

Java is used for full-on applications development on both the client and server side. Javascript is primarily used to make web pages interactive (although it's being adopted for scripting in a number of other environments as well). There's a HUGE difference. Please keep this in mind.

Whatever you do, don't confuse the two when you're around professional Java developers or you'll look like a hapless noob. It's a faux pas, the sort of thing that causes more knowledgeable people around you to look at their shoes and grin.

Chapter 2: Java Variables and Data Types:

In chapter 1, I gave you an initial glossary of terms as a sort of preview for the material we'll be covering in the rest of the book. In this chapter, we'll discuss some basic but critical topics: how variables are declared, created, and destroyed, what types of variables are available in Java, and how you can organize and work with simple sets of variables.

Let's begin by discussing how variables are **declared** (created) and **initialized** (given an initial value), how they pass in and out of **scope** (the part of your code in which a variable is accessible), and how to recover memory when you're done using a reference variable (this isn't necessary with primitives). You can think of this trio of concepts as birth, life, and death if you're as morbid as I am. We'll begin at the beginning: declaring a variable and giving it a value.

Declaring and Initializing Variables:

Taking the simpler case of Java primitives first, there are two ways to declare a primitive variable; the first just declares it, and the second declares it and assigns a value to it at the same time.

Example 1: Declaring a primitive, no assignment:
int aSingleNumber;

Example 2: Declaring a primitive with assignment:
int anotherNumber = 10;

In example 1, we declared a variable of type "int" (an integer) and we didn't give it a starting value. The default value for integers is 0.

In example 2, we declared another variable of type "int" and we initialized it with a starting value of 10.

That's all there is to creating primitives; you declare them, and optionally give them a value. Their variables are directly associated with the value, and can be considered to contain it. Now let's look at reference variables.

Reference variables are a bit more complicated than primitives; unlike a primitive, a reference variable *doesn't* directly hold a value. Instead, it contains a reference to a memory location where an object is stored. This arrangement is called a "**Hard Reference**" and it works exactly like a pointer in C or C++, only it's been streamlined significantly for you.

Remember from chapter 1 that a class is just a blueprint; when you instantiate it, it becomes an object in memory, and your reference variables refer to it. The following examples illustrate how to declare and instantiate reference variables using Strings as a particularly useful example:

Example 3: Declaring a String object without assignment.
String someString;

Example 4: Declaring a String with assignment (assigning an existing object someOtherString to someString; afterwards, both reference variables refer to the same object in memory)
String someString = someOtherString;

Chapter 2: Java Variables & Data Types   Phil's Java Tutorial

Example 5: Declaring a whole NEW string using the "new" keyword, and passing it a starting value via its constructor:

String someString = new String("Something or other");

Example 6: Using "new" but passing it another object (this copies the other object, resulting in TWO Strings):

String someString = new String (someOtherString);

Example 7: Strings are special; you can declare them and assign a value as if they were primitives, even though they're not (this works similarly to using "new"):

String someString = "Something else";

In example 3, we're simply declaring a String without initializing it or instantiating an object.

In example 4, we're declaring a String and initializing it by assigning another String to it. This doesn't create a second String, however; it assigns the reference contained in someOtherString to someString, because reference variables only contain references to objects in memory. Here the reference is copied, and the two Strings point at the same object in memory (thus someString is an alias for someOtherString).

In example 5, we create a whole new String using the "new" keyword; this instantiates a new String object and uses the text in quotes as a starting value for it.

In example 6, we do the same thing as in example 5, but this time instead of using text in double quotes to initialize our String, we're using another String object. This works in exactly the same way; a whole new String is created, using the String we pass in as a starting value. Instead of an alias, we get a whole new String.

Finally, we have example 7. Strings are special in Java, in that you can pretend they're primitives and instantiate a String object using assignment, instead of using "new". The reason this works is that in Java, text in double quotes is automatically created as a temporary String object in memory by the Java runtime. This temporary object's scope is initially limited to the statement in which it appears, but since we're assigning it to a String variable, we're creating a reference to it and thus, it ceases to be temporary.

Now that we've discussed birth, let's discuss life, i.e. a variable's scope.

Variable Scope:

In Java, variables are considered to have a certain "**scope**", which is defined as the region in your code within which a variable exists and can be used. In general, variables are usable everywhere within the block of code in which they are declared. You can declare a variable in any block of code you want, but it will ONLY be visible in that block and blocks contained by that block. When your program moves out of that block of code, the Java runtime considers the variable to be "**out of scope**" and marks it for garbage collection .

For example, let's say you have a variable "foo" declared in your outermost block of code. You have an inner block of code which also declares a variable named "foo". Your outer foo is set to the string "A" and your inner foo is set to the string "B". If your program is currently in the inner block, as far as it is concerned, foo is set to "B". As soon as it passes back into the outer block, the inner foo is forgotten, and the outer foo is once again in use, so foo is once again "A". Here's an example:

Example 11: Scope of foo:

```
{
  String foo = "A";
  {
    String foo = "B";
```

```
    // foo is "B" now, the outer foo cannot be seen
    // because we've created a new foo here.

    {
        // foo is still "B" here. This block is contained in the
        // other one, so the inner foo is still in scope.
    }
}
// foo is "A" again now, the inner foo has passed out of
// scope.
}
```

Scope also comes into play when you call a method. Each method has its own scope, that of the code block that encloses the method's code. When you call a method, you're taken OUT of your current scope and placed into the method's scope -- the method's scope is NOT considered to be contained within the calling code's scope. When the method finishes its work and returns you to the calling code, you will leave the method scope and be returned to the calling code's scope.

Technically, when a reference variable passes out of scope, the reference to its object in memory is broken and the object becomes eligible for garbage collection. However, don't trust this! You might have other references to an object that you've overlooked, leading to a memory leak. You should always take charge of scoping issues and null out any reference variables you're not using. We discuss this in the next section.

We've covered birth and life, so let's move on to death.

Disposing of Objects You Don't Need Anymore:

Because reference variables only contain references to objects in memory, you have to know how to allow Java's garbage collection to reclaim memory when you're done with it. Deliberately setting a reference variable equal to the special value **null** (literally nothing) breaks its reference and makes the underlying object available for garbage collection. In Java, we say you're **disposing** of your objects when you do this. Once set to null, a reference variable is considered to be in an uninitialized state.

It's important to understand that garbage collection (also called gc) doesn't work continuously; it intermittently checks all the objects known about by the runtime to see if they have any references pointing at them. When gc notices that an object has no references pointing at it, it frees that object's memory for use. There may be some delay between nulling out a reference variable and actually getting the memory back. Try not to use too much memory, and don't count on garbage collection to cover for inefficient coding. Here's an example of how to dispose of a String:

Example 8: Setting a reference variable to the special value "null" to dispose of it (make it available for garbage collection):
someString = null;

An important caveat here is that with many objects, you must take additional steps before you null them out or you'll end up with serious problems.

For example, let's say you have a database connection open. If you just null it out, it might hold the connection open on the database side until the garbage collector finally remembers to delete it, or worse, when it times out on the database side. That's going to severely piss off your Database Administrator. Objects like this need to be properly closed down when you're done with them -- you need to close out any connections the object has open, THEN null it out.

Another caveat is that if you've created multiple aliases for an object, you might not remember to null them all out. For example, let's say you have a string called someString, and you've also assigned it to anotherString. You're done with someString, so you do the following:

Example 9: trying to clear out an object you don't need, but forgetting about your other reference variable:
someString = null;

The other variable, anotherString, is still a reference to the string in memory, so garbage collection won't clear out the string. In cases like these, you need to null out both reference variables:

Example 10: clearing out an object with two references:
someString = null;

anotherString = null;

If you fail to null out your reference variables when you're done with them, you run the risk of setting up memory leaks that will degrade performance and possibly crash your software. Be careful and always set your reference variables to null when you're done with them.

Now that we've covered the basic life cycle of a Java variable, let's get into some discussion of the variables themselves. We'll start with the easiest case, that of Java primitives. There are a number of primitives available to you.

Java Primitives:

We'll start with integers, since they're the simplest of the primitive types. An integer is basically just a positive or negative whole number, like 125 or -30. Java offers four data types for holding integers, which differ in size (in bytes) and the range of values they can hold. Going from smallest to biggest:

A "**byte**" is a one byte integer whose values range from -128 (-2^8) through 127 ($2^8 - 1$). The "-1" in the high range is because 0 counts as one of the possible values. I don't use bytes very often, although when I'm trying to work with a binary file, they come in VERY handy for holding individual bytes of data.

A "**short**" is a two byte integer whose values range from -32,768 (-2^{16}) through 32,767 ($2^{16} - 1$). Again, 0 counts as one of the values. I can't think of any uses for short off the top of my head; I generally just use int. Which brings us to...

An "**int**" is a four byte integer whose values range from (-2^{32}) through ($2^{32} - 1$). You'll almost always use ints for your whole number needs. Except when you need a much BIGGER number, at which time you'll use a long.

A "**long**" is an eight byte integer whose values range from (-2^{64}) through ($2^{64} - 1$). This is useful (for instance) when you've got to work with number-only IDs that have lots of digits. There are times when it's impractical to use strings for this sort of thing, and longs can be very helpful.

To declare and use one of these variables, just use the right data type and give it a number that'll fit in it. Incidentally, when you type a number in Java, like 123, by default it's assumed to be an int. If you want it to be considered a long, you can append an "L" to the number, like this: "12424522333L". If you want to feed one of these variables octal or hex values, just precede the number by a zero (for octal), like "076" or a zero and an x (for hex), like "0xA5".

Example 12: Declaring and assigning a long:
long someLong = 18472572842L;

Now let's talk about fractional numbers, called "real numbers" by mathematicians. A real number is any number that can be represented by a fraction. In Java, the data types used to hold reals are "**float**" and "**double**". Floats use four bytes; doubles use eight. In a float, 1 bit is used for sign, 8 bits are used for the exponent and 23 bits are used for the number itself. In a double, 1 bit is used for the sign, 11 bits are used for the exponent and 52 bits are used for the number. All of this, put together, means that floats and doubles are pretty big, big enough that you generally won't have to even care how big they can get. Still, just in case you DO care, I looked them up online and in a book, comparing the answers I got. Here they are:

Float range: 1.17549435E-38 through 3.4028235E+38

Double range: 2.2250738585072014E-308
through 1.7976931348623157E+308

Bottom line here is, if you're generating numbers so big they won't fit in a float, try a double. If they won't fit in a double, you'd better check Google to try and figure out a better way of doing whatever it is you're doing. Note that you're not supposed to use floats or doubles for currency. Java offers **java.math.BigDecimal** specifically for that purpose; you can look it up in the API ref that you should have downloaded with your Java Development Kit (check the chapter on tools for more info).

Note: decimal numbers are always considered doubles by default, so if you're assigning one to a float, you should put a lowercase "f" at the end of the number.

Example 13: Declaring and assigning a value to a float:
float someFloat = 1256.73f;   // remember the "f"!

A "**Char**" is a variable that can represent any 16-bit Unicode character, like 'A', '1', or '\n' (newline). Clearly this makes chars two bytes long. You assign a char like this:

Example 14: Declaring and assigning a value to a char:
char someChar = 'A';

Finally, we have the "**boolean**" which is simply a true or false value. This one's important because it's used in control structures like if statements (we'll see those later). For now, just remember that it's purely true or false. For you C programmers, booleans are NOT 1 or 0 values in Java. They literally contain the special values **true** or **false**.

Example 15: Declaring and assigning a value to a boolean:
boolean someBoolean = true;

So, that wraps it up for the primitives. Everything else in Java is a reference variable that refers to an object. Let's move along now, to our next topic: what happens when you assign a variable of one type to a variable of another.

Assignment Between Different Data Types:

Let's say you have two variables, one long and one int. You want to pass the int to the long. Doing this has almost no effect, because a long has enough room to hold an int. You might do something like this:

Example 16: Assigning an int to a long:

int someInt = 125;

long someLong;

someLong = someInt;

What if you tried to go the other way? Well, if you're SURE that your long will "fit" in an int (it's not too large a number to be held by an int variable) you can assign it to the int without any trouble. You just have to perform an **explicit cast**, "**demoting**" the long to an int for the purposes of the variable assignment:

Example 17: Assigning a long to an int with a cast:

int someInt;

long someLong = 525L;

someInt = (int)someLong; // *this "casts" the long to an int.*

The cast doesn't change the variable someLong; rather, it tells the Java system to consider the value to be an int when it passes it to someInt. You can do this with ANY primitive variable; it's called "**demotion**". The only caveat is when the long is too big to fit in the int. In that case, the long is reduced in size so it will fit in the int (essentially, a long is 64 bits, and an int is 32 bits, so the long is truncated to 32 bits to fit in the int variable, i.e. restricted to the maximum integer size).

Strictly speaking, you can cast any primitive to any other primitive, but you don't HAVE to when the assignment is guaranteed to fit, like when you're assigning an int to a long. You only have to do an explicit cast when you're putting something bigger into something smaller, like a double into a float.

Object Wrappers for Primitives

There are times when you'll want to treat primitives as objects. For example, let's say you want to store primitives in a Collection (an object capable of holding and organizing sets of other objects). This won't work; a Collection will only hold objects. You should use an object wrapper to hold your primitive so the Collection will be able to work with it.

Each primitive comes with an associated object wrapper whose name is the full name of the primitive type with the first letter capitalized. We're going to use the "**Integer**" object wrapper as an example; the others (Float, Double, etc) all work the same way. Consider the following example, which uses integers:

Example 18: Creating an Integer object from a primitive:

int someIntPrimitive = 10;   // *this primitive will serve as our example.*
Integer someInt = new Integer(someIntPrimitive); // *using a primitive.*
Integer anotherInt = new Integer(10); // *using an actual number.*

That's all it takes. Just create a new Integer object and instantiate it using your primitive int, or a raw number. This is useful all by itself, because now you can store someInt in a collection. But that's not all that makes object wrappers useful or interesting.

Why Object Wrappers are Particularly Useful:

These object wrappers are interesting in that they have a lot of **static** members and methods. This means you can use these object wrappers in two ways: you can use them to wrap a primitive for use as an object, and you can ALSO use them as general tools for working with your data. You'll be using them for the latter more often than the former.

Here, for your use, is a list of the static methods and members you might find useful in the various object wrappers for primitives.

USEFUL STATIC METHODS/MEMBERS OF THE OBJECT WRAPPERS:

```
// NOTE: Don't worry about "exceptions" just yet, I"ll explain them in the
// error handling chapter. Just make a mental note of them. Also, if
// you're having trouble with the function-calling syntax, just check
// out the next chapter, "methods", and then come back. Depending
// on your background, this might make sense right away (or not).

// NOTE 2: booleans are just true/false values. This section doesn't
// apply to them.

// Integer, Byte, Short, and Long all contain a "decode" function.
// decode accepts a string and turns it into a number, IF it is actually
// a number. If it isn't, it throws a NumberFormatException. Here's an
// integer example:
int x = Integer.decode(someString);

// All primitive wrappers contain a toString function.
// toString accepts a primitive and turns it into a string.
// Here's an integer example:
String x = Integer.toString(someIntPrimitive);

// All primitive wrappers contain valueOf functions.
// valueOf accepts either a primitive or a String, and returns
// an object holding the correct value. If the String doesn't
// contain the right type of data, of course, you'll get an exception.
// For example, if you use the following but your string isn't a number,
// you'll get a NumberFormatException.
Integer x = Integer.valueOf(someIntPrimitive);
Integer y = Integer.valueOf(someString);

// All primitives have max and min value constants. For example,
// in Integer, MAX_VALUE is just the largest possible int ($2^{31}-1$), and
// MIN_VALUE is the smallest ($-2^{31}$).
// These are static constants, not methods.
int i = Integer.MAX_VALUE;
int j = Integer.MIN_VALUE;

// Floats and Doubles don't have a "decode" function like the integer
// data types. Instead, they have a "parse" function. For example,
// for Float objects, you use parseFloat to pull a float value from a
// String:
float x = Float.parseFloat(someString);

// Doubles would use parseDouble, of course.
//Ints and Longs offer parseInt and parseLong.
```

Now let's move along and consider Strings and StringBuffers. You can't do much of anything in Java without these two objects, so you'll get a lot of use out of the next section.

Strings:

So, now let's get into a little more detail about the most important data type in Java.

As I said in the definitions chapter, a String is an object that contains some text. Since each character in a string is a unicode character, Strings can contain just about anything you could imagine yourself writing using a word processor, whether your native language is English or not. In a general sense, a String is like an array of characters, with the first character being its zeroth one. Because of the way it's been designed, Strings are SO much more useful than that.

Earlier in this chapter, we used String as our example when we talked about instantiating objects and assigning them to reference variables. Take a moment, go back, and review that for a bit. It's very straightforward.

One thing you should know about Strings is this: Strings are IMMUTABLE. This means that once you create a String, you cannot change it. If you assign a new value to a String variable, you are actually creating a whole new String – the old String will be garbage collected as soon as all references to it have been deleted.

NOTE: if you're going to be adding to a String more than several times (for example, building it up over a period of time from chunks of text), for efficiency reasons you'll want to use a different class called "StringBuffer", which I'll tell you about after we're done with Strings. Don't bother using a StringBuffer if all you're doing is altering a String you've already put together! The text processing methods in String are a lot better than the ones in StringBuffer. Just use StringBuffer when you're initially building a String from numerous chunks of text.

Strings are also special in that whenever you put some text between double quotes, you create a temporary String object that Java treats exactly like a String object held in a variable. To see this in action, let's do something completely pointless:

Example 26: Double-Quoted Text as Temporary String:

int howLong = "ThisIsAnExample".length();

What we did there was call the "length" method of the temporary String the Java runtime created to hold "ThisIsAnExample". So, remember that every time you use double-quoted text in your code, you're actually creating a full-fledged String object to hold it.

Because String has been specifically designed to hold text, it offers a number of very useful text-processing methods. On the next couple of pages, I'll show you how to use some of the more important ones. When you get a chance, you'll want to look over the String entry in the API reference as well, just to see what's available. Usually, you'll just end up using one of the methods I'm about to tell you about, but occasionally, you might find yourself doing something unusual that requires a bit more. It pays to be familiar with String.

HOW TO WORK WITH STRING OBJECTS:

How to determine a String's length (for length, counting starts at 1, not 0 – in other words, the zeroth element is counted as element #1 and length is an actual character count):

int howLong = someString.length();

How to add two Strings together to produce a third, concatenated String:

// Adding Strings together to form new Strings is called **"concatenation"**. Here's how it works.

String firstString = "test";

String secondString = " of concatenation";

String thirdString = firstString + secondString;

// thirdString now equals "test of concatenation".

This also works with temporary Strings, and multiple Strings:

String thirdString = firstString + " PLUS " + secondString;

// thirdString now equals "test PLUS of concatenation".

Another way to concatenate Strings:

// Usually, you'll just use the "+" operator above, but this works too:

String firstString = "test";

String secondString = " of concatenation";

String thirdString = firstString.concat(secondString);

// thirdString now equals "test of concatenation".

How to create a new String that is an all-uppercase version of another String:

String uppercaseString = sourceString.toUpperCase();

How to create a new String that is an all-lowercase version of another String:

String lowercaseString = sourceString.toLowerCase();

How to create a new String using a part of another String (a "substring").

// Here, let's use the example string "Manual" and assume we want to pull "ua" from it. The
// syntax of the substring method is:

String resultString = sourceString.substring(beginindex, endindex);

// Here, Java will start with the character at beginindex, and copy all characters up to
// endindex – 1. The length of the returned String is endindex – beginindex. Also, Java starts
// counting characters at 0 as it moves through the String, so in the String "Manual", "M" is
// character 0, "a" is 1, and so on. Returning to our example, let's pull "ua" from "Manual":

String resultString = sourceString.substring(3,5);

Alternate version: How to get a substring starting at an index and going all the way to the end of the String:

// If you just want the last four characters (for example) of a String, just pass a single index –
// the start position. Using our previous example, let's get "nual" from "Manual" (again, "M"
// is the zeroth character, "a" the 1st, "n" the 2nd):

String resultString = sourceString.substring(2);

How to split a String on some character you've decided upon as a delimiter:

// Sometimes you'll want to break a String into chunks, dividing it by some special character
// (called a "delimiter") you've decided upon. The most common delimiters people choose are
// vertical bars ("|"), semicolons, and commas. In order to do this, use the "split" method. In
// this example, sourceString is comma delimited. Note that the split method returns an
// array.

String [ ] resultStrings = sourceString.split(",");

How to compare one String to another String:

// Tricky! Remember, Strings are objects, which are held in reference variables! If you just try
// to compare one String to another directly, you'll end up comparing the memory addresses
// of the two objects, which will never be equal.

// The first approach you'll want to use is the "equals" method. This simply returns a boolean
// "true" or "false" which tells you whether two strings are equal (i.e. have the same exact set of // characters in them). For example,

boolean areTheyEqual = stringOne.equals(stringTwo);

// While using this approach, you might want to compare the two Strings without considering // case (uppercase or lowercase characters in the Strings). To do that, use equalsIgnoreCase,
// like this:

boolean areTheyEqual = stringOne.equalsIgnoreCase(stringTwo);

// A second approach is to use the method "compareTo" to see whether the two Strings are
// equal or different. This function returns a negative number if the first String is less than the
// second, a positive number if the first String is greater than the second, and a zero if the two
// Strings are equal.

// Now, when I say one String is "greater than" another, I don't mean that in a mathematical
// sense. I mean it in a "**lexicographical**" sense. Pretend you're sorting the Strings
// alphabetically. If stringOne comes before stringTwo, it is less than String two. If stringOne
// comes after stringTwo, it is greater. Consider this example:

String stringOne = "Aardvark";

String stringTwo = "Apple";

String stringThree = "Petunia";

String stringFour = new String(stringOne);

int comparison;

comparison = stringOne.compareTo(stringTwo);   // result: -1.

comparison = stringThree.compareTo(stringTwo);   // result: +1.

comparison = stringOne.compareTo(stringFour);   // result: 0 (they're the same)

// Of course, you can use compareTo while ignoring case, just as you did with equals. Just use
// "compareToIgnoreCase", like this:

comparison = stringOne.compareToIgnoreCase(stringTwo);

// Now, we're going to look at several methods for searching a string to find a sub-string. In all // of the following methods, please assume that the following two lines of code have been run
// already. They just set up the variables mentioned in the examples:

String containingString = "Now is the time for all good men...";

int position;

How to see if one String is contained within another String -- indexOf:

// The first way you can check whether one String is contained within another is using the
// plain "indexOf" method. This will return an integer showing the character position at
// which the search String occurs within the larger String (or, -1 if it's not found). For
// example:

String searchString = "time";

position = containingString.indexOf(searchString);   // position of "time" is 11.

How to see if one String is contained within another String -- indexOf with starting point:

// You can also use a second form of indexOf to start your search at a specific point in the
// String, say, halfway through. For example, let's find the first "o" after character 10.

String searchString = "o";

position = containingString.indexOf(searchString, 10);   // position of "o" is 17

How to see if one String is contained within another String -- lastIndexOf:

// Maybe you want to see the index of the LAST place where a String occurs within a String (or
// -1 if it's not found). Let's see where the last "o" is in our main String.

String searchString = "o";

position = containingString.lastIndexOf(searchString);   // last position of "o" is 26.

How to see if one String is contained within another String -- lastIndexOf with starting point:

// Let's try something else. Let's try a second form of lastIndexOf, and find the last position for
// "o" in the string that is BEFORE position 10.

String searchString = "o";

position = containingString.lastIndexOf(searchString, 10);   // last position of "o" is 1

How to fetch a character at a specific position in the String:

// Sometimes you might want to parse through a String, doing something with the individual
// characters in it. Or maybe the third character of a specific String always holds an error
// code. Or something else you want to use. Here's how to fetch a character at a specific point
// in a String.

String containingString = "This is a test of a character fetch.";

char fetchedChar;

fetchedChar = containingString.charAt(5);   // "i" is returned.

How to replace all instances of a character with another character:

// Sometimes you want to clean out all instances of a specific character from your Strings.
// Maybe you want to clean out all carriage returns. Maybe you don't like the letter "x".
// Whatever. Here's how to do it; this first form accepts two characters.

String containingString = "1 800 555 1212";

char replaceChar = ' ';

char newChar = '-';

containingString = containingString.replace(replaceChar, newChar);

// containingString has been changed to "1-800-555-1212".

How to replace all instances of a substring with another substring:

// Here's a second form, which uses Strings. This is more useful, because you can make the
// Strings anything you want, up to and including empty Strings (if you want to strip
// characters out of your String). ACTUALLY, the type it uses is "charsequence" which is an
// interface implemented by String (and some other types). We talk about interfaces in the
// objects chapter. For now, just realize that you can pass this method Strings, and that makes // it WAY more useful than the character version:

String containingString = "Now is the time for all good men...";

String replaceString = "Now";

String newString = "Soon";

containingString = containingString.replace(replaceString, newString);

// containingString is now "Soon is the time for all good men...";

StringBuffers:

Now, I mentioned that if you're going to be adding to a String a number of times, for example reading lines from a file and tacking them onto the end of a String variable, you probably don't want to use it as a String while you do. Strings are immutable, so every time you want to add something you have to create a whole new String. Your old Strings have to wait to be garbage collected, which makes your software take up more RAM while it's running. The solution is to use a StringBuffer while you're adding to the String, and then move the data to a String once you're done.

There are a few ways to instantiate a StringBuffer: you can pass it nothing, in which case it'll be empty and have a default starting capacity; you can pass it a String, in which case it'll have a default value and a starting capacity based on the size of the String; and you can pass it an integer, in which case it'll be empty and have the specified starting capacity. There's another way to set it up if you're using Java 1.5 or later, but don't worry about that one; if you really must, you can look it up in the API reference. You'll almost always be using the first three methods below.

Declaring and instantiating a StringBuffer:

// The following three methods are the main ones you'll want to use to instantiate a
// StringBuffer.

// Method 1:   Just create a StringBuffer and worry about adding things to it later.

StringBuffer firstOne = new StringBuffer( );

// Method 2:   Create a StringBuffer with an initial value (a starting String). You can either use // a literal String in double quotes or a String object. The StringBuffer will start out
// containing that String as its initial value. The first line of code below uses a literal, the next
// two use a String object.

StringBuffer secondOne = new StringBuffer("Starting Value!");

String tempString = "Starting Value";

StringBuffer thirdOne = new StringBuffer(tempString);

// Method 3:   Create a StringBuffer while specifying an initial starting capacity as an integer. // Note that this capacity is measured in characters, and will grow as you add new Strings to
// the StringBuffer. This is primarily useful if you know that a StringBuffer is going to be close
// to a specific size, and you want to ready it in advance.

StringBuffer fourthOne = new StringBuffer(100);

Once you've created your StringBuffer, you'll want to append text to it until the body of text is more or less complete, then call toString() to create a String version of your text, and finally, use some of the more powerful methods in String to perform any final adjustments. One thing I always use a String object (*instead* of a StringBuffer) for is text replacement. While both String and StringBuffer offer a "replace" function, the one in String is FAR more useful than the one in StringBuffer. In fact, the one in StringBuffer is pretty primitive in comparison. You don't even get any efficiency out of using the StringBuffer version, because it ends up returning a StringBuffer object so you have the same memory considerations you would have with String.

HOW TO WORK WITH STRINGBUFFERS:

Most of the methods in StringBuffer are EXACTLY the same as an equivalent version in String. Specifically, StringBuffer offers "charAt", "indexOf", "lastIndexOf", "length", and "substring". Since the syntax and usage is basically IDENTICAL to that of the equivalents in String, I won't repeat them here. I'd rather just talk about things specific to your use of StringBuffer.

How to append Strings to your StringBuffer:

// You can "append" any primitive (or primitive wrapper class) to your StringBuffer, as well
// as any String or any other StringBuffer. When you do, the value you're appending is not
// affected. It is merely copied into the StringBuffer. There's even an append function for
// "Object" so if one of your objects has a toString method defined, you can append that as
// well. Note that Java 1.5 and 1.6 also allow you to append "charSequence" objects. Again,
// you can find that one in the API ref.

exampleStringBuffer.append("This adds a String.");   // Adding a String.

exampleStringBuffer.append(someString);   // Adding a String object.

exampleStringBuffer.append(someString + someOtherString);   // Adding while concatenating.

char [ ] aCharArray = { 'a', 'b', 'c', 'd', 'e' };   // a char array for our example...

exampleStringBuffer.append(aCharArray);   // This adds an array of characters.

How to copy your StringBuffer into a String when you're done changing it:

// StringBuffer offers you a toString method so that when you're done altering your String you
// can hand it back off to a regular, immutable String object. I know that String (and every
// other Object) has a toString method, and I said I was only going to talk about things specific // to StringBuffer.
However, I want to mention this here because you'll almost always end up
// calling it at least once. Here's an example; I'm declaring a string called "doneAltering" to
// receive the StringBuffer data.

String doneAltering;

doneAltering = exampleStringBuffer.toString();

How to reverse all the text in your StringBuffer:

// StringBuffer offers the reverse() function, which creates a new StringBuffer that is the exact
// reverse of your current StringBuffer. In other words, if your StringBuffer contains "ABCDE"
// and you call reverse on it, the new StringBuffer you create will contain "EDCBA".

StringBuffer newStringBuffer = exampleStringBuffer.reverse();

That wraps it up for Strings and Stringbuffers. Now let's move on to sets of variables, and how you can work with them. For now, we'll just look at the relatively simple Array and the enumeration. Later on in the book, there'll be a chapter on "Collections" which are much more powerful; this material will be easier to follow once you've read the chapter on object oriented programming.

Arrays:

When we want to store a set of primitives or objects (and they are all of the same exact type), we can use an **"array"**. Think of an array as a simple, ordered list of whatever data type you've declared it to hold. Things you have put in the array are called its **"elements"**, and their position within the array is identified by an integer called the array **"index"** (alternately, it has also been called its **"subscript"**). In Java, all array **"indices"** (the plural of index) start at zero (0) and count upwards one element at a time. Given an array of 10 elements, the index of the first element is 0 and that of the last element is 9.

Java's array syntax is pretty simple; you just declare a variable of the data type you want and use square brackets to indicate that you're declaring an array instead of a single variable. If you want, you can initialize the array with a set of values separated by commas and surrounded by curly brackets. Alternately, you can instantiate an array using the "new" keyword and give it a specific size without putting anything in it at first.

Technically, arrays are objects (hence the use of the new keyword). They all offer the member variable "length" which tells you how many elements are in the array. NOTE: This length is counted starting at 1, not 0, and is an actual count of the number of elements. Don't confuse it with the array index!

Here are some examples that should give you an idea of how arrays work. in practice, you won't use arrays that often (except when doing things like splitting Strings) because Java offers much better ways of handling sets. Consider these examples:

Example 19: Declaring an array to hold integers and giving it 10 values:
// (note that since we're supplying ten values initially, the array will permanently have
// a length of 10)
int [ ] myIntArray = {0,1,2,3,4,5,6,7,8,9};

Example 20: Declaring an array to hold 10 integers, but not giving it any values yet:
int [ ] myIntArray = new int[10];

Example 21: Declaring an array as a placeholder, for an array you'll instantiate later on:
// Sometimes you'll want to declare an array but not put anything in it. For example, you
// might want to call a method later on that returns an array, so for now you're just creating a
// variable to hold it. This is pretty common.

int [ ] myIntArray;

Example 22: Putting values in an array we have declared:
// Note that we're accessing individual positions in the array using an index in square
// brackets, and that the indexing on an array starts at zero (0). Note that you cannot
// place a value in a position that doesn't exist; make sure your array is large enough
// to hold whatever you intend to put in it.

myIntArray[0] = 0;
myIntArray[1] = 1;

Example 23: Fetching a value from the fifth position in an array:
// Again, we start counting positions from 0.

int someInt = myIntArray[4];

Example 24: Declaring a multidimensional array of int:
// This example shows that you can create an array that contains arrays. In this two
// dimensional (2-D) case, the indexing is like a grid, with rows and columns. Note that the
// number of rows can be different from the number of columns. Note also that you're not
// limited to 2-D arrays. You can go completely nuts and have arrays of arrays of arrays. I
// can't think of any situations in which you'd want to have more than a 3-D array, or maybe
// 4-D if you're measuring x, y, and z coordinates, plus time, but then I'm pretty boring as
// programmers go.

int [ ] [ ] my2DIntArray = new int [10][5];

my2DIntArray[0][0] = 1; // Row 0, column 0

my2DIntArray[3][5] = 3; // Row 3, column 5

Example 25: Declaring and initializing a 2-D array of int:
// I've never seen anybody DO this, but you COULD; basically you'd be creating an array of
// two arrays (think "rows"), and then populating both of them with values. The outer curly
// brackets in the first line below is for the "array of arrays"; the two sets of inner curly brackets // are for the
arrays it contains:

int [ ] [ ] my2DIntArray = { {1, 2, 3, 4, 5, 6}, {0, 1, 5, 4, 2, 3} };

int test1 = my2DIntArray[0][3];   // test1 = 4

int test2 = my2DIntArray[1][2];   // test2 = 5

int test3 = my2DIntArray[0].length; // test3 = 6

// Note in this last line, we accessed the first array (array 0) as an object, and called on its
// length property to see how many elements (arrays) it contained. Remember, arrays are
// objects, and you can treat them as such.

Enumerations (collections of constants):

People familiar with C or C++ will know about the "enum", which is basically just an array of Strings in which each String is associated with a numeric index. Java offers enumerations, which provide the same construct. It's always used in more or less the same way. You have a list of constants that sensibly map to some set of numbers. The typical examples of this are the days of the week (Monday = 0, Tuesday = 1, and so on through Sunday = 6) and the months of the year (January = 0, February = 1, and so on until December = 11). Using enumerations lets you use String constants with a switch statement, basically. Here's the syntax on how to create one:

Example: How to create an enum (a Java enumeration):

```
enum Weekdays{ Monday, Tuesday, Wednesday, Thursday, Friday, Saturday, Sunday }
Weekdays  selectedWeekday;   // Create an enum variable for a chosen weekday...
selectedWeekday = Weekdays.Wednesday;   // At some point you set the variable's value.
if(selectedWeekday = Weekdays.Monday){
    // just for example, using it in an "if"
}
// Another simple example using a switch statement...
switch(selectedWeekday){
    case (Weekdays.Monday):
        // Some code here
        break;
    case (Weekdays.Tuesday):
        // some code here
        break;
}
```

One Last Note: Access Modifiers:

Access modifiers define how a Java class, method, or variable can be accessed. In this discussion, we're just going to talk about variables, but the ideas we discuss will ALSO apply equally well to methods (aka functions), classes, and interfaces.

Starting with the most common access modifier, "**public**" means that the variable it applies to can be accessed from within the same class and from outside it as well (any code that instantiates a copy of the class can access that variable). Think of it as "wide-open". Public is the default access level if you don't explicitly state which one you want.

Next up, but very important, is "**protected**", which means that the variable it applies to can be accessed from within the same class or any class derived from it. If another class inherits the class the variable is in, that class can access the variable. We haven't discussed this too much yet; I'll go into more detail in the "classes and objects" chapter. For now, just think of protected as the best non-public access level you can give to your work. It's also friendly towards your coworkers, because it lets them access your class members in their derived classes.

Next, we have "**private**" which means the variable can ONLY be accessed within the same class in which it is defined. Nothing outside that class' code block can access the variable. Note that using "private" is NOT friendly to your coworkers, so you should try to use it only in places where you're doing something complicated that's really easy to botch (so you're trying to protect them from themselves rather than just being a control freak).

Finally, there's "**package**" which I'll have to explain more fully in the classes and objects chapter. For now, think of a package as a set of related classes; package access means that any object in the same set can access the variable or method.

Any variable can be declared using one of these access modifiers. It's very simple; it looks like this:

Example of a private int variable:

private int someInt;

That's enough on this topic for now. We'll revisit it soon, touching briefly on it again in the "methods" discussion in the next chapter, and in more detail in the "classes and objects" chapter.

Chapter 3: Syntax, Conditional Statements, Looping, and Methods

In this chapter, we'll move along to the actual programming constructs of Java. By constructs I mean things like flow control (looping), conditional statements (if/then) and simple math using variables. These constructs exist in every modern programming language; they've evolved over the past fifty years, starting with COBOL and Fortran, proceeding through Pascal, Smalltalk, C and C++, to the present with Java and Microsoft's dot net languages. If you know these in one language, you (almost) know them in every language; all that remains is learning the syntax. Let's start with the simplest constructs, the ones with which you'll do ordinary math.

In Java, math looks and works just like algebra. If you've ever studied algebra, you already know how to program most mathematical operations in Java. One variable accepts the resulting value from some mathematical operation you do with other variables. Consider these examples:

How to do ordinary math in Java:

Addition:
int x;
int y = 20;
int z = 30;
x = y + z;   // *x now equals 50.*

Subtraction:
int x;
int y = 20;
int z = 30;
x = z - y;   // *x now equals 10.*

Multiplication:
int x;
int y = 10;
int z = 5;
x = y * z;   // *An asterisk is the multiplication character. x now equals 50.*

Division:
int x;
int y = 50;
int z = 10;
x = y / z;   // *A slash is the division character. x now equals 5.*

Modulus:
int x;

int y = 53;

int z = 10;

x = y % z;   // A percent sign is the modulus character. x now equals the remainder, 3.

Exponentiation:
int x;

int y = 5;

int z = 2;

x = y ^ z;   // A caret ("^") is the exponentiation character. x now equals 5 squared, or 25.

Incrementation / Decrementation:
x++;   // Increment (increase) x by 1 AFTER the current line is executed.

++x;   // Increment (increase) x by 1 BEFORE the current line is executed.

x--;   // Decrement (decrease) x by 1 AFTER the current line is executed.

--x;   // Decrement (decrease) x by 1 BEFORE the current line is executed.

How to use this (examples):

y = z + --x;   // Decrement x before adding it to z.

y = z + x--;   // Decrement x after adding it to z.

Shorthand for applying a mathematical operation to the same variable that is receiving the value:
x += y;   // Short for "x = x + y"

x -= y;   // Short for "x = x - y"

x *= y;   // Short for "x = x * y"

x /= y;   // Short for "x = x / y"

x %= y;   // Short for "x = x % y"

// The previous set of mathematical functions are more or less the same for all the numerical
// data types. The following set only applies to floats and doubles, not to integers.

Truncating:
// To truncate a float, just assign it to an integer or a long. Java will automatically truncate it
// (cut off its decimal digits) and assign the truncated value to the int (the float, of course, is
// not affected):

int x;

float y = 5.5;

x = (int) y;   // x now equals 5, y is still 5.5.

Rounding, Ceiling, and Floor:

// In order to do rounding, you'll want to import the package **java.lang.math**. It offers
// round(), which rounds numbers normally, ceil() which always rounds numbers up, and
// floor() which always rounds them down. Check out these examples:

float x = 5.3;

float y = 5.5;

float z = 5.6;

float result;

result = Math.round(x);   // result = 5.0

result = Math.round(y);   // result = 6.0

result = Math.round(z);   // result = 6.0

result = Math.ceil(x);   // result = 6.0

result = Math.floor(z);   // result = 5.0

In addition to what you've seen in the examples, java.lang.math offers a generous supply of math-related functions, so you should definitely check it out in the API reference. If you're going to be doing something that involves math, before you code it yourself, try to look it up in this package. It might already be a part of the language.

Order of Precedence:

Before we go any further, we should talk about "order of precedence". When you have a complicated statement with a number of operations in it, Java decides what to do first using its order of precedence rules. Generally these work just as they do in Algebra. Operations that have equal precedence are carried out from left to right within a statement, and groups of operations with higher precedence are carried out first.

Think of the process this way: for each level of precedence, starting with the highest and proceeding towards the lowest, the Java runtime will move through the statement from left to right, carrying out all operations at that precedence level. I don't know whether they've actually implemented it that way at the system level, but effectively, this is what's happening.

Let's try a deliberately simple mathematical statement, just to get the gist of how this works. We'll "bench test" it (run through it on paper instead of on a computer). Our statement is:

result = 5 + 12 - 2 * 4 + 10 / 2 + 4 * 3;

Note that the left side of the equals sign contains a variable which will be receiving a value; the right side of the equals sign contains an "**expression**" which will return a value to the variable.

Let's parse through the expression the way Java will, and see what value Java will come up with. The first thing we're going to do is carry out the multiplications and divisions, moving from left to right along the line. So, the statement gets transformed this way, first:

result = 5 + 12 - **2 * 4** + **10 / 2** + **4 * 3**;

result = 5 + 12 - **8** + **5** + **12**;

Since the remainder of the operations are at the same level of precedence (they're all addition or subtraction) Java will move through them all from left to right, and end up with a resulting value of 28. Pretty simple, right?

Use of Parenthesis to Control Order of Operations:

If you want to exert a little more control over the order in which parts of a statement are carried out, you can use parenthesis to break the statement up into logical pieces. Each pair of parenthesis, composed of an open "(" and a close ")" parenthesis, is considered to represent a specific level of precedence within the statement. Pairs of parenthesis contain expressions, which in turn can contain other pairs of parenthesis. Expressions like this are evaluated starting with the innermost parenthesis and working outward, with operations at the same level of precedence being evaluated from left to right.

You have a lot of freedom in creating statements this way; as long as you pay attention to the order of operations you're setting up, you can do some pretty complex stuff. Let's go back to our last example, but parenthesize it in two different ways:

First, here's the unparenthesized statement:

result = 5 + 12 – 2 * 4 + 10 / 2 + 4 * 3;

If you just want to obey the built-in Java order of precedence, but for some reason want to be explicit about it, you could do this:

result = 5 + 12 – (2 * 4) + (10 / 2) + (4 * 3);   // *result is 28.*

But what if the calculation required that you do some of the additions first? The result would be totally different. You could use parenthesis to change the order of operations:

result = (5 + 12) – 2 * (4 + 10) / 2 + (4 * 3);   // *result is 15.*

Let's run through that one a step at a time and see what's going on:

result = (5 + 12) – 2 * (4 + 10) / 2 + (4 * 3);
result = (17) – 2 * (14) / 2 + (12);
result = (17) – 28 / 2 + (12);
result = (17) – 14 + (12);   // *result is 15*

If you wanted to carry out the operations in a third, different order, you could use even more parentheses and group like this:

result = ((5 + 12 – 2) * (4 + 10)) /((2 + 4) * 3);   // *result is 11.66*

This one would be carried out like this (running one step at a time again):

result = ((5 + 12 – 2) * (4 + 10)) / ((2 + 4) * 3);
result = ((15) * (14)) / ((6) * 3);
result = 210 / 18;   // result = 11.66

In general, it's a pretty good idea to use parenthesis to explicitly control the order in which your expressions are evaluated. It's always best to avoid having to rely on your memory of Java's rules of precedence. It also makes your code more readable to people who have to maintain it later.

Having said that, I can't leave you hanging without actually telling you what the order of precedence rules are. So, here are Java's order of precedence rules. Operations corresponding to a higher order of precedence are carried out before operations at a lower order of precedence (provided there are no parenthesis forcing a different order). In the following list, the first rule is at the highest order of precedence, the second is the next highest, and so on down to the lowest. I looked this information up at Sun Microsystems website; it should be pretty trustworthy.

Java's Order of Precedence Rules:

This table contains a list of order of precedence rules you can use to evaluate statements with. The way this works is simple. For each level of precedence, read a Java statement from left to right and carry out all operations that correspond to that level. Continue working your way down through the levels of precedence until all of the operations have been carried out. In the following table, "myVar" just means a variable of some type (it could be an int, whatever).

Java's Order of Precedence Rules, listed from highest to lowest:

Postfix:	myVar++, myVar--
Prefix, Unary:	++myVar, --myVar, +myVar, -myVar, !, ~
Multiplication, division, modulus:	*, /, %
Addition, subtraction:	+, -
Shifting:	<<, >>, >>>
Boolean:	<, >, <=, >=, instanceOf
Equality:	==, !=
Bitwise and:	&
Bitwise or:	^
Bitwise inclusive or:	|
Logical and:	&&
Logical or:	||
Ternary:	? :
Assignment:	=, +=, -=, *=, /=, %=, &=, ^=, |=, <<=, >>=, >>>=

Note that you may not have seen all of these operators just yet; this list of precedence rules is a reference. You'll recognize a lot of it from algebra, and parts you don't recognize may turn up later on in the book. Other items like bit shifting (">>", "<<", ">>>") and the bitwise operations ("&", "|") are more obscure and most programmers will rarely need to use them, so I don't cover them in this book.

That covers order of precedence, so let's move on and look at conditional statements.

<u>*Conditional Statements:*</u>

Conditional statements allow you to choose between different courses of action based on the value of a condition the statements test. In Java, there are three basic non-looping conditional statements available. There is the "if" statement, the "switch" statement, and a third statement using something called a "**ternary operator**" that acts as a sort of shortcut. In this section, I'll show you the syntax of each of these. I'll also try to provide you with a useful example.

Before we get into the three types of conditional statements, we have to mention that the "**condition**" in a "**conditional statement**" is a specialized type of expression that produces only a **true** or **false** value. The conditional statement will carry out one set of actions if the expression is true and another if the expression is false.

Because all conditions evaluate to boolean true/false values, you will almost always be doing some form of comparison. Is a value greater or less than another, equal to another, or within a certain range of possible values? So you'll have to think in these terms. In other words, if you want to create effective conditional statements, you'll have to get used to breaking things down, no matter how complicated, into sets of expressions that ultimately result in a "true of false" answer.

Conditions generally follow the following form:

<u>*Syntax of Java contitions:*</u>
((**expression1**) **operator** (**expression2**))

// For example,

(inputNumber >= oldNumber)

// Or,

((inputNumber * 3) <= (oldNumber * 2))

Here, you can see that we're comparing two expressions using a conditional operator. The statement as a whole (containing both expressions and the operator) must evaluate to either "true" or "false". Each individual expression can have any value you want, as long as the comparison is valid.

You can also build complicated, compound conditions using multiple expressions. In this case you wrap them in parenthesis and link them with an "and" or an "or" operator. I'll give you some examples in a sec, but first, let's talk about the comparison operators.

In Java, you may use combinations of the following **comparison operators** to create your conditional statements. **Note that these are primarily for Java primitives**; if you are comparing one object to another, you cannot use comparison operators because object variables only contain memory locations, not values. When comparing objects, you should use any built-in comparison methods the objects' designers have provided you with. You should be able to find out about these using the API reference if the object is part of Java itself, or the object's documentation. A good programmer will usually include at least an "equals" method if an object needs to be compared to another of the same type.

In the following table, first I've named an operator, then posed a question, then demonstrated how you would use an operator to answer that question. In each case except for the last three (which work on boolean expressions, not values), I've used example values "value1" and "value2". Note that the last example is totally different, because the "not" operator just reverses the value of whatever statement it's applied to. Let's proceed.

List of Comparison Operators Available in Java (along with what they mean):

// Equality ("=="):   Is value1 equal to value2?

(**value1** == **value2**)

// Inequality ("!="):   Is value1 NOT equal to value2?

(**value1** != **value2**)

// Greater than (">"):   Is value1 greater than value2?

(**value1** > **value2**)

// Greater than or equal to (">="):   Is value1 greater than or equal to value2?

(**value1** >= **value2**)

// Less than ("<"):   Is value1 less than value2?

(**value1** < **value2**)

// Less than or equal to ("<="):   Is value1 less than or equal to value2?

(**value1** <= **value2**)

// Logical And ("&&"):   Are expression1 AND expression2 both true?

((**expression1**) && (**expression2**))

// Logical OR ("||"):   Is either expression1 OR expression2 (OR both 1 and 2) true?

((**expression1**) || (**expression2**))

// Logical NOT ("!"):   If expression1 is true, return false. If expression1 is false, return true.

(! (**expression1**))

Now for some examples. In the following examples, we'll use four integer variables, number1, number2, number3 and number4. Assume number1 = 5, number2 = 10, number3 = 15, and number4 = 20. First, let's look at the simplest case, two expressions and one comparison:

(number1 > number2)   (FALSE)

(number1 < number2)   (TRUE)

((number1 + number2) <= number3)   (TRUE)

Now let's look at a slightly more complex condition, using and and or statements:

((number1 > number2) && (number3 < number4)) (FALSE)

((number1 > number2) || (number3 < number4))(TRUE)

((number1 < number2) && (number3 > number4))   (FALSE)

Here's something important: Java performs "**short-circuit**" evaluation. This means that in the first example above, since number1 isn't greater than number2, the whole "and" expression must be false, so Java stops right there. The second expression is never evaluated.

In the third example above, the first expression IS true, so Java has to evaluate the entire expression to find out whether it's false as a whole. So in this case, the entire expression IS evaluated.

Chapter 3: Syntax, Conditional Statements, Looping, and Methods

That's pretty much all there is to conditions. You'll be using them throughout the rest of this section, so try to get used to them. Now let's move on to the simplest of conditional statements, the "if" statement.

<u>***The "IF" Statement:***</u>

Now that we've looked at the sort of expressions we can evaluate, let's look at the "if" statement. It has a few forms, but the simplest form just tests a single expression (the **condition**) and if it is true, carries out the rest of the statement following the condition, all on one line. The syntax works like this:

<u>*Syntax of the simplest "if" statement:*</u>
if(`condition`) `statement` ;
// For example:
if (x > y) z = x;

In this example, if the value of x is greater than that of y, we're going to assign its value to z. This is about as simple as it gets. Note that the next more complicated form of the "if" statement replaces the part of the statement after the condition with a block of code:

<u>*Syntax of an "if" statement with a code block:*</u>
if(`condition`) {
    // do something
}
// For example:
if (x > y) {
    z = x;
}

Note that if we've included a code block, we don't include the trailing semicolon. Statements that include blocks don't require the semicolon; the end of the block ends the statement. Now let's demonstrate an "if" statement with an alternative – something we want to do if the condition is false. For this, we use an "else" clause, and the whole statement is called an "if/else":

<u>*Syntax of an "if" statement with an "else" clause:*</u>
if (`condition`) {
    // do something
} else {
    // do something else
}
For example,
if(x > y) {
    z = x;
} else {

```
    z = y;
}
```

Notice that now, if the condition isn't true, we've carried out the code in the second block.

There's one more form of the "if" statement that is very useful. This uses a set of "else if" clauses which have their own tests. It lets you test a number of conditions sequentially, using a final "else" clause as a default (in case none of the conditions were true). You can use as many else if clauses as you want; I'm only using one to save space. The syntax is:

Syntax of an "if" with "else if" and "else" clauses:

if (<u>condition</u>) {

    // do something

} else if (<u>condition</u>) {

    // do something else

} else {

    // do something by default

}

// For example:

```
if ( partNumber == 49 ) {
    partName = "Main Assembly";
} else if ( partNumber == 136 ) {
    partName =  "Rear Assembly";
} else {
    partName = "unknown";
}
```

That about wraps it up for the "if" statement. You might have noticed that if you're in a situation where you have a really long set of "else if" clauses, it might be nice to have another statement that simplifies the coding a bit. We do, sort of, but it's not that useful because it has too many restrictions. It's called the "**Switch**" statement.

The Switch Statement (testing against multiple values):

The next conditional statement we're going to talk about is called the "Switch" statement. It lets you compare an integer or char (or one of a few other primitives like byte) to a set of numeric or char values and perform a different action depending on which value the variable matches. It's basically like a large "if" statement with a number of "else if" clauses. However, I don't find the switch statement too useful; I prefer the broad "anything goes" feel of an if statement, where you can specify any condition you want to without limitations. For me, switch feels too constrained, too formal... But that's a matter of taste.

Regardless... You might find yourself in a situation in which being able to select from a number of integers or chars (for example) could actually be useful. So, here's the syntax, and an example:

Syntax of the Java Switch Statement:

Switch (<u>integer variable</u>) {   // *parenthesis are required.*

    case <u>possible value</u> :

        // *do something*

        break;

    case <u>another possible value</u> :

        // *do something else*

        break;

    case <u>another possible value</u> :

        // *do another thing*

        break;

    default:

        // *put your default action here (like an "else" clause)*

}

Note: the "break" statements above are necessary so you stop processing at that point, once you've done whatever you're supposed to do in that case. If you want Java to "fall through" more than one case, you can omit the break statement from that case and the next one will be executed as well, until you put in a break statement or the Switch statement ends.

Example of Switch Statement:

Switch (myIDNumber) {

    case 10:

        myIDString = "ten";

        break;

    case 20:

        myIDString = "twenty";

        break;

    default:

        myIDString = "undefined";

}

    Of course, any Switch statement can be easily replaced with an if/else if/else statement, and offer you more functionality and flexibility.

    The last conditional statement we'll discuss, the ternary operator, is basically a shortcut. It lets you create a very, very terse expression returning the maximum of two values.

Java's Ternary Operator ("?"):

    Ok, honestly I can't think of any time I've actually used this one in my code. However, it's interesting, and can be useful, so I'm going to show it to you. Basically, you would want to use this operator when a variable needs to be assigned one of two values based on whether a condition is true or false. Here's the syntax of this sort of statement, followed by an example:

Syntax of a statement using the Java ternary operator:
`destination variable` = (`condition`)? `value1` : `value2`;
// For example:
livesDowntown = (city.equals("Albany"))? true: false;

Isn't that interesting? If you've got a very simple condition and you don't feel like typing, you can write a rather short statement to evaluate it. Again, I really don't get a lot of use out of this. I generally stick with if/else statements.

Now, let's move along to the next topic involving conditional expressions, namely, that of repeated execution of code based on a condition, i.e. "**looping**". Java offers three distinct types of looping statements, and all three are useful. We'll start with the simplest, the "**While**" loop. Looping is very simple; basically you're just going to repeat a set of code until some condition is no longer true.

The While Loop:

The while loop is very simple, and extraordinarily important. You'll use it all the time. Essentially, a while loop lets you run a block of code over and over again until the condition associated with it is false. Of course, this means you have to make sure that the condition actually does become false at some point, or you'll have an "**infinite loop**" (your program will appear to hang while it's stuck in your loop, until you get fed up and kill the program at the O/S level). Some people do this deliberately, using the number "1" as their condition. Don't do that. Always create a condition that is based on something that changes inside the while loop. Note that each run through a loop's code block is called an "**iteration**". Looping over a set of data is also called iteration. While you loop, you're "iterating".

Let's start with the basic syntax; then I'll tell you about some statements you can use to change how your loop works while it's running (the "break" and "continue" statements).

Syntax of a While Loop:
```
while ( condition ) {
    // do something
}
// For example:
int number = 1;
int factorial = 1;
while( number <= 5 ) {
    factorial *= number++ ;
}
```

That was a kind of dumb, boring example, just calculating 5 * 4 * 3 * 2 * 1, but it demonstrates the basic syntax of the while loop. Note that the main characteristic of a while loop is that it will run until its condition is false. This means that it might not run at all if the condition is false in the beginning.

If you want to "break out" of a while loop while it's running, you can use the "**break**" statement. This will break you out of the while loop and resume processing on the next statement after the while loop's code block. It looks just like this:

Syntax of the break statement:
break;

If you want to skip the rest of the while loop's code block for one iteration and go straight back up to the loop's condition, use the "**continue**" statement. It looks like this:

Syntax of the continue statement:
continue;

Break and continue are pretty important, especially if you're looping over some data from a database or web service. For instance, you might use continue to skip some of the data you're not interested in, i.e. if the record relates to a closed account, you'd "continue" past it. Or you might use break to stop looping over the data altogether if you detect something wrong with it, like maybe none of the records are the proper length. A lot of this is really about error handling.

There's one more potentially useful thing you can do. You can break based on a "label", i.e. you can select which while loop you're breaking if you've nested more than one. To do this, you put the label before the while loop you want to break out of. Then, you use an alternate syntax for break:

Syntax Example of Break or Continue With a Label:
```
label name 1:
while (condition1) {
    label name 2:
    while (condition2) {
        if (condition3) {
            break Label name 1;
        } else if (condition4) {
            break label name 2;
        }
    }
}
// Here's an example, albeit a very simple one, that'll break all the way out when B = 4.
mainLabel:
while(A++ < 10){
    while(B++ < 5){
        if(B == 4){
            break mainLabel;
        }
```

> }
> }

    I haven't personally used that very often. You'd generally only want to use it if some condition in a nested loop required you to break all the way out of the whole nested loop at once.

    Now that we've discussed the while loop, let's look at the "**do-while**" loop. The do-while loop checks its condition *after* it's run its block of code, so the code will always be executed *at least once* no matter *what* the condition evaluates to. Here's the syntax of the do-while loop:

Syntax of the do-while loop:

do {

    // do something

} while (condition);   *// Note the trailing semicolon!*

// For example:
int number = 1;
int factorial = 1;
do {
    factorial *= number++ ;
} while(number <= 5);

    Note that you can use break and continue with a do-while loop in exactly the same way as with a while loop. They're essentially the same looping construct, with the only difference being that the while loop is a "**pre-test**" loop and the do-while is a "**post-test**" loop.

    These two while loops are actually more than enough for anyone's looping purposes, but Java offers one more type of loop. You can use a "for" loop whenever you know exactly how many times you want the loop to run. This comes in handy when you're working with any fixed number of things, like a fixed array of strings split from some larger string, or a known number of database records.

    A for loop uses a different type of condition than while loops do; it has three parts separated by semicolons. The first part initializes the loop control variables, the second part contains the actual condition that will be tested, and the third part increments (or decrements) the loop control variables. You will almost always use integers as your loop control variables, and you will almost always use a condition that checks the size of the integers. However, note that you are not limited in what you can use as your condition. You can use pretty much anything, with one caveat: try not to write code that's so weird your coworkers learn to hate and fear you; it's bad form. Here's the syntax of the for loop:

Syntax of the for loop:

for (variable init ; condition ; variable increment) {

    // do something

}

// For example:
int i = 1;

```
int factorial = 1;
for ( i = 1;  i <=5;  i++) {
    factorial = factorial * i;
}
```

That's pretty much all there is to the for loop, other than to mention that **just as with the while and the do-while, you can use break and continue to change its execution.**

I should point out that you can initialize, test, and increment more than one variable at a time. Usually you'll only be working with one loop control variable, but really, you're not limited to one. Just separate them by commas (except the condition in the middle, which MUST be one and only one expression). Consider this example:

Example of a ridiculous for loop with more than one control variable:

```
for (i = 0, j = 0, k = 1; ( (i < 5) && (j < 3) && (k < 20) ); i++, j++, k+=3) {
    // just an example
}
```

You won't have to do anything like that very OFTEN, but it's nice to know that you can if you want to. Another thing I'd like to bring up, because it comes up all the time, is the use of a nested for loop. The typical way you'd use this is to iterate over all the elements of a two dimensional array. The first array would be considered to contain rows, and the second array would be considered to contain columns. Traditionally, you would deal with this problem using two integer indexes, "i" and "j" for row and column data respectively. Your for loop would look something like this:

Example of a for loop with a nested for loop:

```
// (assume you have 100 rows of 10 strings each):
int i, j;
for ( i = 0;  i < 100;  i++) {
    for ( j = 0;  j < 10; j++) {
        // do something
    }
}
```

Remember, you can nest any code block inside any other code block. Whiles can be nested, do-whiles can, anything can, really. By the way, it's traditional to use the letters i, j, k (and so on) for loop control variables. This goes all the way back to Fortran programming and most professional programmers will expect you to write your code this way. You can name your loop control variables anything you want, of course, but it's nice to obey conventions like this.

Methods (aka Functions):

Every programming language has some sort of function or procedure syntax which lets you take a chunk of code that's frequently used and associate it with a name you can call as a shortcut. It's common sense, really.

Instead of having to rewrite the same code over and over again, you can wrap it in a method and simply call it by name. If you should ever have to change the code, you only have to change it in the method implementation, and wherever it's called, the new version will be used.

Methods are the building blocks of all modern 3GL (third generation) languages. Ever since the 1970's, when "structured programming" became widespread, programmers have been breaking their code up into methods and gathering those methods into libraries. When object oriented programming became popular in the 1980's, it arose as a further refinement of structured programming that divided code up further, into logical "objects" that owned data and methods that acted on that data.

In Java, all methods are declared within the code block of a Java class. They have several parts, including an access modifier (public, private, etc), the optional "static" keyword, the optional "final" keyword, a return value (the data type your method will return, if any), a name, a list of parameters in parenthesis, and a code block. Here are examples for the syntax:

Syntax of a Java Method Declaration:

// Note -- there's also a "throws" keyword, which we'll handle a little later, in the
// error handling section, and a method can be static, final, or both.

```
access modifier return type method name (parameter list){
```
// method body -- with a "return(value);" statement if you're returning a value.
}

Example of a Java method declaration that doesn't return a value:

public void helloWorld (String extraMessage) {

    system.out.println("Hello, World! " + extraMessage);

}

Example of a Java method declaration that returns a String:

public String helloWorld(String extraMessage){

    return("Hello, World! " + extraMessage);

}

Example of a Static Java method declaration:

public static void sayHello ( ) {

    system.out.println("Hello, World!");

}

Example of a Final Java method declaration:

// Note that this is very antisocial! Nobody will be able to override your method!
public final void sayWhat( ) {

    system.out.println("What?");

}

The first part of the method declaration is the access modifier. Remember our discussion of access modifiers in the previous chapter? They apply to methods in the exact same way they apply to variables. For example, a public method can be accessed from outside the class, and a protected method can be accessed only by the class itself and classes derived from that class. So the first part of a method declaration is the access modifier. If you don't specify one, the default access modifier is "public".

Next, you can optionally add the word "static". If you do, then the method will be available even if you haven't yet instantiated the class the method belongs to. What this is used for is if you want to use a class as a sort of function library, so people can import the class (or its package) and call static methods within it. You'll see this a lot in the Java standard library. A good example of it is the primitive wrappers, all of which offer a number of static functions for working with data (we looked at some of those earlier).

The next part of a method declaration is the data type the method returns. If your method will be returning a value, like a String, you have to explicitly state what data type that value will be. If your method will be returning nothing at all, you have to use the keyword "**void**" as your data type. Void just means "I'm returning nothing". If you declare your method with a return value, you MUST use a "return" statement (as in the second example) to return a value of the right type or you'll get a compilation error.

Next up is the method name. Method names start with lowercase letters and can contain any combination of lowercase, uppercase, underscores, and numbers. Traditionally, in Java, we don't use underscores. We start with a lowercase letter and we use uppercase letters for the first letter of each following word. This is called "camel case" in a lot of circles because it resembles a camel's humped back. It looks like this: "someMethodIMadeUp". You should try to make your method names describe as succinctly as possible what the method actually does. But don't get carried away; if your method names are more than around 30 characters long, you're going too far.

After the method name, you must declare the data types and names of the variables that will accept the input data for the method, separating them with commas. Let's go off on a brief tangent and talk about "call by value" and "call by reference".

Traditionally, there were two ways of calling a function: by value, and by reference. When you call a function by value, the variables you pass into the function are copied locally in the function's code block, and the original variables aren't touched. This is a very safe way to call a function; it has no "side effects" -- the function just does what it's supposed to and nothing else happens. Usually, functions that were called by value returned a value, so this is traditionally called "call by value – return".

Call by reference, on the other hand, passes variables into a function in such a way that the function doesn't copy them locally; it works on the original variables instead. Calling by reference opens you up to side effects because you can inadvertently alter the variables you pass into the function, as well as doing whatever the function itself was supposed to do. This is sometimes what you want, but if you do it by accident, it can gum up the works, producing hard to find bugs and irritating the hell out of your fellow programmers.

In Java, *technically* all variables are passed by value. However, since a reference variable only contains a reference to an object in memory, the value that is passed to a method is NOT the object you want to pass to it, but a reference to that object. In other words, the method is following the reference and working on the original object, NOT a copy. The result is that when you pass a reference variable to a method, you're passing it by reference, not by value, *even though all Java variables are technically passed by value*. So this is something you have to keep in mind while working on your methods – don't let side effects happen unless you INTEND them to happen -- don't alter the reference variables you pass in to your methods unless you really want to alter them permanently.

Note: *if you DO want an object to be passed by value, you have to take some additional steps involving the interface "cloneable" and this is mildly involved, but nothing to worry about (we'll talk about it in the objects chapter, where I'll give you instructions).*

Here are two examples of methods that ought to give you the general idea. The first one just returns the longer of two strings, and the second figures out the volume of a cube.

Example of two methods that return a value:

```
public String longerString( String first, String second) {
    if( first.length( ) > second.length( ) )    {
        return(first);   // This is a reference to first, not a new String.
    } else {
        return(second);  // This is a reference to second, not a new String.
    }
```

```
}
public int volumeOfCube( int width, int height, int depth ) {
    int volume;
    volume = width * height * depth;  // primitives are passed by value; these are copies.
    return(volume);
}
```

Note that a function can contain any sort of Java code you'd like to put in it, including variable declarations, code, calls to other functions, and so on. Next let's talk about how you actually use ("**call**") your methods. There are two ways of calling a method, and which one you use depends on whether the method returns a value or not.

If the method returns a value, you can call the method from within a condition or statement, and use the value of the method in some way (like testing it against a value in the condition, or passing it to a variable). This is how this looks:

Examples of using a method call within a condition or statement:

```
// This first example calls a function inside a condition:
if ( readTheLineCount( ) > 50) {
    // just an example
}
// This second example just passes the return value of the function to a variable:
int currentLineCount = readTheLineCount( );
```

The second way of calling a function is just to call it as a statement by itself. Usually you'll do this with functions whose return type is void. Strictly speaking, you can do this with functions that return values also, but you usually wouldn't want to because it would be like throwing their return value away.

Example of issuing a method call by itself:

```
refreshFileContents();
```

As long as the function's access modifier lets you interact with it, you should be able to call it and use it. Note that if you declare a function as having a non-void return value, you MUST return a value with the correct data type at some point or the function won't even compile.

Chapter 4: Classes, Objects, and Interfaces (OOP).

In this chapter, first we're going to take a conceptual look at what object oriented programming is all about, working through a completely nontechnical example. I think this might be helpful for those of you who are coming from a non-OO background; if you're comfortable with OOP you can skip ahead. Then, we're going to look at the syntax Java uses for OOP, and I'm going to show you all the constructs you'll need to know. This includes Java classes, abstract classes, and interfaces. While I'm at it, I'll tell you how I go about designing my own work, which you might find interesting, or at least amusing.

Preview of OOP: A Purely Conceptual Look to Get You Started:

If you've read the "Preliminary Concepts" chapter, you already have an idea of what Java objects are: they're memory constructs that contain all data and methods related to some specific real-world concept. For example, you might have a "Person" object which works with data related to the employees of your company, or you might have an "Order" object which stores and processes information related to sales orders.

You also know what classes are; they are the blueprints from which objects are constructed. You start out by writing code in a class file, and when it's compiled and used in someone's software, it is used to generate objects of that type.

Try to remember this: in a formal sense, classes are source code, and objects are compiled code running in memory (or cached on a server). The two terms are often used interchangeably by experienced programmers, because their meaning is clear from its context. If they're talking about a running program, it's understood that they're talking about objects, and if they're talking about source code, it's understood that they're talking about classes. It's harmless, informal, and friendly, but it confuses people who are new to Java.

Now let's talk about how you should actually think about your objects while you design them.

If you want to be as efficient as possible, you shouldn't design an object only as a one-time, specialized thing; you should always assume you're going to be extending and reusing it for years after you initially build it. For example, a "Person" object never represents JUST a person; it can represent a security guard, a secretary, an executive... And over time, it'll represent new types of people that might not even exist yet, as new job titles are created within a company. You should account for the certainty of this sort of evolution when you design the object in the FIRST place. ASSUME that everything will change over time. ASSUME that your object hierarchy will have to grow to encompass possibilities you haven't even thought of yet. In your initial design, try to account only for the most general of characteristics and capabilities, leaving room for additional ones to be added in later, in derived classes. In other words, start the design process with an abstract base class that takes into account everything you can identify that is totally common and generic to the type of object the class represents.

Going back to our "Person" example, this would include things that all people have in common, like their names, home telephone numbers, work numbers, email addresses, home address, and office location. It would also include methods that all people could perform, like "getBirthdateAsString". The idea is to start out with the most general possible version of a class, on the assumption that you'll be extending it to specialize it later on.

Let's consider a more interesting example. Pretend you want to model an automobile in code (assume you're a videogame programmer working on a racing game). You might model a car by starting out with a base class called "StandardModel" and design it to simulate an ordinary four cylinder engine, a cheap automatic transmission, four doors, four seats, and finally, a standard set of controls including a steering wheel, brake, gas pedal, and transmission shift lever. Everything about this car would be generic and normal. Windows, unibody construction, the works.

You'll want to design a programmer's interface for the class, so that programmers using it will know how to interact with it. Your "Interface" will list all the public functions available to programmers, including things like "addFuel", "startDriving", "drive" and "hitTheBrakes". Thanks to this interface, from the perspective of a programmer *using* your StandardModel class it's a black box with a set of functions he can use. He shouldn't know, nor should he care, about the code you wrote to make those functions available.

Another programmer might extend this class to create two new derived classes, each of which inherit all of the characteristics of your base class and implement your interface. He might call them "StandardModelAuto" and "StandardModelManual". The first one is a little more expensive than your default and has a somewhat more effective automatic transmission capable of 120 mph (yours was only good for 100 mph). The second one is equipped with a manual racing transmission and costs a player more money, but has steel gears so it won't burn out as quickly, and lets him drive faster while cornering. The programmer writes the code simulating all this, including customized versions of the "startDriving" and "drive" methods defined in the interface, and hands it to his supervisor.

A third programmer is writing the code that actually *uses* the classes your team is working on. He uses a "StandardModel" variable to hold car objects because they're all derived from your StandardModel base. He writes his code so that if the player in the game only has the default model, the software will assign a StandardModel object to the variable. If the player has bought a better transmission, the software will assign one of the two other models of car to the variable. Now, no matter what type of car object the variable is holding, this software can call the startDriving and drive methods and the right version of them will be called automatically -- the Java runtime keeps track of what type of object a variable actually holds. This is great for the programmer, because he doesn't have to write any special code; he writes one set of code based on the interface for StandardModel. The only time he has to write anything specific is at the point when he assigns the object to his variable in the first place.

Think about how nicely this works out. The developers don't have to know anything about each other's code. All they have to know is that the entire set of objects based on StandardModel use the same interface.

This is what is meant by "encapsulation, inheritance, and polymorphism", the three pillars of object oriented programming. The objects based on StandardModel are encapsulated because they contain all their data and the methods that act on that data, and don't rely on anything external to do their work. The StandardModelAuto and StandardModelManual objects, being derived from StandardModel, demonstrate inheritance because they inherit all of its characteristics, and can extend or replace some of them. Finally, this situation demonstrates polymorphism because it doesn't matter which object is actually assigned to the StandardModel variable, when you call the "drive" method the correct version of that method will be called by the Java runtime.

This is what working in Java is all about. You spend a lot of time up front, designing a class hierarchy that will represent the real-world concepts you're working with. You move from the most general to the most specific, and you design your code for extensibility and maintainability. Your aim is to write code that is as reusable as possible, and to share that code with your coworkers so you can all gang up on a project. The idea is that any given programmer in an organization should only have to solve a problem once. All he has to do is share his solution with the rest of the team, and they can incorporate it into their own work (even extending and adjusting it).

Sounds good, right? Let's look at some syntax.

The Syntax for Declaring Regular Classes:

In Java, every class should be placed in its own file, and the filename should be the same as the class name with a ".java" suffix. If you're designing a "Person" class, you'll save it to a "Person.java" file. Once you compile it, the output file will be named "Person.class". If you've made the class part of a package, it'll be in a subdirectory based on the package name. For example, if you put your Person class in a package called mycompany, your Person.java class will end up being "mycompany/Person.java". Packages can be nested; if you're putting one package inside another, separate them with dots. Nested packages become nested subdirectories. If your package is "mycompany.common", then the Person.java class will end up in "mycompany/common/Person.java". Note that when you compile, the output files end up being generated in the same exact subdirectory setup as your Java source code files. If your package is "mycompany.common" and your source code is in "mycompany/common/Person.java", your output file will be generated in "mycompany/common/Person.class".

By convention, the first letter of every class name, as well as the first letter of each additional word in the name are all capitalized. For example, you might have a class name like "OfficeManager". Package names, on the other hand, use only lowercase letters.

Package names by convention start with your company or personal Internet domain name in reverse. For example, a company whose site URL was "javarelated.stuff.com" would name their packages starting with "com.stuff.javarelated". Because your package names are based on your domain name (which you own), the ownership of your code is automatically documented by this naming convention. It also ensures that your package names are completely unique, even if they're used by people outside your organization.

I used to hate this practice; I thought it overly complicated package names. My thought back then was that you should just use your organization name without the "com" (or "org" or whatever). Over time I've realized that this was a stupid position to take, and I've repented it. Using "com" as a prefix puts your package in the "com" hierarchy, which is where every other Java programmer will expect it to be. This is a GOOD thing, so please do it that way, and forget I ever said anything to the contrary.

Syntax of a Java Class Declaration (including the whole file involved):

package `package name`; *// Specifies the package to which this class belongs.*

import `package name`;   *// Imports a package for use in this class.*

// the following is the most basic way to declare a class; you can also use the "extends"
// keyword to extend another class, or the "implements" keyword to implement an
// interface, but we'll talk about that a little later. Note that all classes are derived from
// "Object" automatically. NOTE: You can make a class "final" (similar to a final variable)
// but this is very antisocial! None of your fellow programmers will be able to extend it!

class `class name` {

    // Class Variable Declarations -- Any variables you need should be declared
    // here, grouped together before your methods. This is by convention. Usually,
    // the access modifier should be "protected" so child classes can access variables.

    // You can leave the variable uninitialized...
    `access modifier` `data type` `variable name`;

    // or set a starting value.
    `access modifier` `data type` `variable name` = `default value`;

    // One or more Constructors, methods named after the class which
    // list no access modifier, and are therefore public by default. The
    // parameter list can be anything any regular method can accept,
    // and you can have more than one constructor as long as their
    // parameter lists are different (see the discussion on signatures
    // later in the chapter).
    `class name` (`parameter list`) {

    }

    // Class Method Declarations -- a set of methods you want to offer to
    // the code that uses this class. Some may be public, others protected
    // or private. You'll generally want to make most "protected" so that
    // child classes can access them. The methods that are "public" will
    // end up being the de-facto interface for the class, because programmers
    // will use them to interact with it.

    `access modifier` `return type` `method name` (`parameter list`) {

        }
}

Example:

package mycompany.common;

// *The following "import" statements make packages we would*
// *like to use available throughout this class. Here, we're importing*
// *everything in java.net and java.io (the asterisk means "all contents").*

import java.net.*;
import java.io.*;

// *And here is the class declaration itself. Note that you follow the name with*
// *a code block. The code block contains all the code for the class.*

class someClass {

    // *First you would declare all variables, giving each an access modifier*
    // *like "public" or "protected". The default is "public". What I do is, if I*
    // *want something to be publicly available, I use "public", otherwise, I*
    // *use "protected" so my child classes can access it.*
    protected String somebodysName = "test";

    // *Next you would declare all methods in the class, giving each an access*
    // *modifier (same as variables). One of the methods must be a constructor,*
    // *which handles the initial setup of the class, including pre-loading any*
    // *variables that haven't already been initialized.*

    // *First, the constructor; since this is an example, we'll leave it empty.*
    // *the constructor is named exactly like the class, with NO RETURN VALUE*
    // *and NO ACCESS MODIFIER:*
    myClass (){

        // *In practice, you'd initialize your variables here.*

    }

    // *Then, a regular method. All the code you add to a class has to be in a method.*
    // *Regular methods must state their return type (here we're returning String);*
    // *if they return nothing, use the type "void".*
    // *NOTE: If you don't put in an access modifier, the default is "public".*

    protected String whatsMyName() {

        return somebodysName;

    }

}

    If you would like to have your class extend another class, you have to change the declaration slightly, and use the "extends" keyword. When you extend another class, you generally either replace methods in the parent class, or you add new methods, or you change or add variables -- basically you're going to create a more specialized version of it:

Syntax for extending another class:

class <u>class name</u> extends <u>parent class name</u> {

    // **Your child-class code goes in here, extending the parent class.**

}

Example:
// In the following, ChildClass (the child class) extends ParentClass (the parent class).
// Because ChildClass is derived from ParentClass, you can store a ChildClass object in
// a ParentClass variable (but not vice versa).

class ChildClass extends ParentClass{

    // you'd write child-class-specific code in here.

}

    By doing this, your class will inherit everything that was in the parent class. Note that if something in the parent class is declared with the access modifiers "public", "protected", or "package" you'll be able to interact with it, including overriding or overloading it. If something in the parent class is declared "private", forget about modifying it. The original programmer didn't want you messing with it, so you can't. My suggestion is that everything in your classes should be "protected", except things you want to allow everyone to use, which should be "public". Note that if you're writing a Java application, your "main" method MUST be public or nobody will be able to start your program.

    Note that when you instantiate your child class, both the child class and the parent class will be instantiated (and its parent, and that ones parent, and so on). This is important for you to understand. You're not just instantiating your child object, although you can only directly refer to it in your code. This has an important implication when it comes to writing the constructor for your child class! You have to initialize not only your child class, but its parent as well! To do this, you use the keyword "**super**" -- this lets you refer to methods in the parent. Here's how to access the parent class' constructor using super:

How to Initialize a Parent Class Using Super, From the Child Class' Constructor:

// Let's say our parent class is "Person" and it has a constructor that lets you pass in
// a person's first name, last name, and phone number. Your child class' constructor
// accepts email address and sets that as well. Here's how the constructor should look,
// assuming the child class is called ITPerson:

ITPerson (String emailAddressIn, String firstNameIn, String lastNameIn, String phoneIn) {

    super (firstNameIn, lastNameIn, phoneIn);
    workEmail = new String (emailAddressIn);

}

Overriding and Overloading Methods:

    In Java, when you design a derived class, you can choose to **override** methods defined in the parent class. To override a method means to entirely replace it. You design a new method that has the same exact "**method signature**" as the parent class' version. A method signature is a combination of the method name, return value, and list of parameters and their types. If your new function has the same return value, name, and parameter list as the parent class's version, your new version will be the one used by the Java runtime when that method is called while your derived object is being stored in a variable of the parent class' type. You can override any method that has been assigned the access modifier "public", "protected", or "package". Note that if you want to call the parent class' version of a method, you can still do so using the keyword "super" as we did with the constructor earlier. For example, to call the parent version of fubar( ), use super.fubar( ).

In Java, you can also "**overload**" a method. This means, you can design multiple versions of the method that have *different* method signatures (you may vary the return value, the parameter list, or both). For instance, within one version of a class, you can design four different versions of its constructor. One might take no parameters, one might take a string, one might take a string and an integer, and one might take a string, an integer, and a boolean. As long as your different versions of the method have different parameter lists, you can make as many versions as you like. This is useful for giving other programmers several ways of setting up an object.

NOTE: Another thing you can do is overload methods between a parent class and a child class, offering more versions of the method in the child class. This can be tricky, however, because the Java runtime will ONLY look at the variable an object is in to determine what methods and members are available. So if you overload a method between a parent class and a child class, and your object is in a parent class variable, the Java runtime will NOT be able to see the overloaded versions of the method! If you want to offer extra versions of a method in a child class, that's great, but you have to store the child class object in a child class variable in order to access them at runtime. You cannot use a parent class variable in this case.

Abstract Base Classes -- Creating a Foundation for a Class hierarchy:

You don't always want to start a class hierarchy with a class a programmer can instantiate. Let's say you're working on a Payroll system, and you've started your class hierarchy with a "Person" class. You've noticed that everyone in the company works within a role, and that whenever a Person is in use by the system, it really ought to be forced to adopt one of the roles you've designed. Each of these roles derives from Person, and you want to make sure that a new programmer doesn't make the mistake of trying to use the Person object directly. In this case, you'd make Person an "abstract base class", because they cannot be directly instantiated; they MUST be extended by another class in order to be used.

In an abstract base class, you can provide variables that will be inherited by child classes. You can also provide methods you want all the child classes to share; your implementation of these methods can be thought of as default versions, used when a child class doesn't provide its own. You can also provide totally abstract methods that only have a method signature; these MUST be implemented by a child class, unless the child class is abstract as well. Finally, you can offer "static final" constants that will be available to all child classes (and other code even when you haven't instantiated an object of this type yet). Similarly, you can offer static, final, and static final methods. *Remember that final methods are somewhat antisocial because your fellow programmers can't override them if they extend your classes.*

An abstract base class is basically like a blueprint designing the general form of all classes within a hierarchy based on it. It's a very good way of beginning your designs. Here's the syntax of an abstract base class:

Syntax of an Abstract Base Class:

// I've left out the package and import statements; they're the same as with a
// regular class, so there's no need to repeat them here. Note that you can use
// "extends" with abstract classes, just as with regular ones. They work just like
// any other class, except for the fact they can't be directly instantiated.

abstract class `class name` {

    // Variable declarations here

    // define some constructors here.

    `class name` ( ) {

        // default constructor, no parameters!

    }

    `class name` (`parameter list`) {

```
        // Overloaded constructor, takes parameters
    }
    // You'd probably have default implementations of several methods here.
    // Now for an abstract method; this MUST be implemented by any child class,
    // unless that child class is abstract too!  Note that it ends with a semicolon.
    // It's ONLY a method signature, with no body.

    access modifier abstract return type method name ( parameter list );
}

// Example:

abstract class employee {

    protected firstName;
    protected lastName;
    protected middleInitial;

    // And so on... pretend I have variables for all the common things people need.

    employee( ){

        // Default  constructor. Let's assume we don't need to do anything for now.

    }


    employee(String firstNameIn, String lastNameIn, stringMiddleInitialIn) {

        // Of course there would be parameters for every member variable...

        firstName = firstNameIn;
        lastName = lastNameIn;
        middleInitial = middleInitialIn;

    }
    protected abstract void configureWorkSchedule( employeeSchedule empScheduleIn );

}
// By the way, note how I keep naming my input variables with an "In" suffix. This
// can be useful, it makes it really obvious in your code which variables are inputs for
// class initialization, It also reminds you to swiftly hand the initial inputs off to member
// variables.
```

Basically, what you're trying to do when designing an abstract base class is set up a base from which you can build any sort of child classes you might want. You should collect all your common functionality in your abstract base class, and add specialized code to your child classes. Note that you can use a variable of the base class type to hold any child class object. Again, only methods and variables defined in the base class will be accessible through a base class variable. Keep this in mind when building your child classes.

One thing you can do is have levels in your hierarchy, at which points you define different sets of functions. For example, lets say you're building objects designed from an abstract base class "Person". There might be one set of methods that make sense for all people, and this set of methods would be designed into Person and inherited by all child classes in the hierarchy. You might also have an abstract child class called "ITPerson" derived from Person. This child class (and its children) might have a bunch of extra methods that don't apply to anyone outside of the IT department.

If you're working with software for H.R. you might use a Person variable to work with Person-derived objects. On the other hand, if you're working with a scheduling system only used by I.T. you might use your ITPerson variable to hold ITPerson-derived objects. Java's flexible; you can even have a situation where your I.T. scheduling system calls out to your H.R. system for something, passes it the same ITPerson object it's been working with, and lets it do some work with it before handing it back. Interestingly, while the H.R. system is working on the object in memory, and sees it as a regular Person object (because of the variable it's storing it in) the I.T. system is STILL pointing at the object with an ITPerson variable, and still sees it as an ITPerson object. The two organizations are interacting with the object in fundamentally different ways. Because the H.R. system doesn't care about I.T. specific methods, it won't matter if the Person variable H.R. knows about can't see them. As long as you pay attention to how the objects are being used, you can get away with this kind of thing. It's pretty neat stuff.

Of course, it helps when you can force your child classes to support a set of methods you've defined. An abstract base class lets you do that in one way, by forcing child classes to provide implementations for abstract methods. But what if you don't need to provide any default variables or implementations of methods? What if you only want to design the set of available functions, and maybe a constant or two? And what if you want to have classes accept multiple groups of these sets of available functions? In that case, you would want to use an "**interface**".

Interfaces and Why They're Useful:

A Java "**interface**" is an absolutely abstract class, containing no actual implementation of methods or non-constant variables. It offers an advantage over abstract classes in that while you can't ever extend more than one class at a time in Java, you CAN "implement" multiple interfaces. This makes a few interesting things possible.

Let's look at an example. One I've been kicking around lately involves processing digital versions of paper forms. Think about this situation:

Pretend that you're supposed to build a system that will process a large number of input files whose data originally came from paper forms and was data-entered by another department. Let's say the forms are stored as XML files when your software receives them. Each form has a different set of fields, although they all relate to a similar set of information. You have no way of knowing in advance which forms an individual user might want to submit. He might submit only one, or a dozen. He could submit the first three form types, the last three, or a random sampling of them. You want to be able to handle this situation in the simplest, cleanest way possible, while writing the absolute least amount of code.

Obviously you're going to design a set of classes that represent all the different available forms. That's already the cleanest way to handle that aspect of the problem. So instead, you look at the main set of code, the one that will be reading in the source data, figuring out which form object to use, and calling the methods that will process the form. You realize that if each form object uses the same exact method calls to process the form, you don't need to know what type of form object it is to process it. You can write only ONE set of code that handles ALL the form objects.

This gives you a side benefit in that you can add new types of forms whenever you want, as long as the method calls are the same. You still have to write a tiny bit of code that chooses and instantiates the right type of object in the first place, but you've made the problem a lot simpler. The trick is to ENFORCE this, to make SURE that each form object offers the correct set of methods.

To make this happen, you design a "dataEnteredForm" interface. In it, you design the set of function calls each data entered form has to offer. Then, you set up each form class so that it implements the dataEnteredForm interface (thus requiring the class to implement all those methods).

In the code that processes the forms, you create a dataEnteredForm variable, and assign it the correct type of form object. This works because you can use an interface variable to hold any object that implements that interface. Of course, you'll only be able to access methods defined in the interface, but that's not a severe limitation here. Finally, you call the set of methods that process the form, without paying attention to what type of form it is.

Over time, as you add new forms, you keep implementing the interface and you hardly have to touch the main body of code -- you just have to add the small piece that puts the correct object in the Interface variable. Thus, your code is pretty simple, but accomplishes something very complicated.

First, let's look at the syntax of an interface; then let's look at the syntax of a class declaration implementing the interface:

Syntax of an interface:

```
// First, declare the interface itself:
interface interface name {

    // Next, declare any constants (note that "static final" is implied automatically,
    // but it helps to explicitly put 'em in -- it makes it clearer what's going on):
    public static final variable type variable name = value;


    // Then, set up the signature for any methods your classes will have to implement:
    abstract return type method name ( method parameters );

}
// Example:
interface TalkingInGibberish{
    public static final String gibberish = "bleaaargh";
    abstract String gimmeSomeGibberish();
}
```

Syntax of a class that implements an Interface:

```
// The class declaration uses the implements keyword:
class class name  implements  interface name {
    // You MUST implement the methods in the interface in
    // the body of your class.
}
// Example:
class LocalGibberish implements TalkingInGibberish{
    public String gimmeSomeGibberish(){
        return(gibberish);
    }
}
```

It's pretty easy to set an interface up. It's mostly a matter of planning, figuring out what you're going to need in advance and defining it up front. Note that I'm not suggesting you go back to the bad old way of doing things with Big Up Front Design (BUFD) the "waterfall method" way... You can use agile methods with this approach, just make sure you finish your interface design and the classes you're going to use it with before you move on to other things. Get them tested and approved first, so you know you won't have to rework all the code depending on that interface later on.

NOTE: interfaces can extend other interfaces, just like classes can extend other classes. Also, classes that implement interfaces can extend other classes. Just mix and match:

Syntax of interfaces that extend other interfaces:

```
interface interface name  extends  interface name {
    // The rest is the same
}
```

// Example:

interface Foo extends Bar{

}

Syntax of a class that implements an interface AND extends another class:

class `class name` extends `class name` implements `interface name` {

   // the rest is the same

}

// Example:

class Foo extends Bar implements Snafu{

}

Syntax of a class that implements more than one interface and extends another class:

class `class name` extends `class name` implements `interface1`, `interface2` {

   // Still the same

}

// Example:

class Foo extends Bar implements Snafu,AwCrap{

}

Abstract Base Classes Vs. Interfaces:

To sum up with respect to abstract base classes and interfaces, the rule of thumb I like to follow is simple:

If you're designing an object hierarchy in which there's going to be at least some common code among all the objects, use an abstract base class to hold all the common functionality and define a set of abstract methods you'll implement in your child classes. Make sure you push as much of your object's functionality as you can into the abstract base class; it'll make maintenance a lot easier (you'll only have to debug one set of code, and won't have to hunt around your child classes for whatever's causing you trouble). Try to make sure the only code in your child classes is that which differentiates them. Keep them simple. Obviously I prefer the abstract base class approach because it lends itself to this sort of organization.

If you're designing an object hierarchy in which the code will always be different, i.e. the same set of actions have to be taken by all objects, but each object will end up defining its own way of doing those actions, use an interface. I don't prefer this approach, because in terms of long-term maintenance, as the number of classes in your hierarchy grows, making changes to common chunks of code becomes much more difficult. Sometimes you have no choice.

The two approaches are both important; you should use the one that best suits a given situation.

Call by Reference/Call by Value Redux: SHALLOW COPY / DEEP COPY

If you remember, in an earlier chapter we saw that all reference variables hold is a memory address to an object in memory, so even though *technically* they're passed by value in methods, they're still effectively passed by reference. We also mentioned that there was a way around this using the Java interface "cloneable". Let's talk about that now.

The interface "cloneable" doesn't actually contain any methods. It's basically like an on/off switch; by implementing it, your class indicates to the Java runtime that it wishes to cooperate in cloning. The actual

Phil's Java Tutorial — Chapter 4: Classes, Objects, and Interfaces (OOP)

"clone()" method you'll use to clone objects is a part of the Object class, from which all objects (even yours) are ultimately derived, but this method always returns an "Object" type. Usually you'll override clone() to return an object of the right type, and in your overridden version, you'll call super.clone() and cast it to the right object type before returning it (you'll see in the examples).

Cloning, in the Java Object sense, is a "shallow copy" operation. It creates a new copy of an object, bit for bit. This copies all of the primitive data perfectly, but reference variables held in the object are still only references to the same objects in memory. Strings, for example, will end up shared between the old copy of the object and the new copy.

Sometimes this is ok, and a shallow copy is all you want. If this is the case, all you have to do to clone an object is:

A. *Implement cloneable*
B. *When you intend to pass the object by value instead of reference, just call the ".clone()" method of your object and pass the result instead of the object itself.*

If the object isn't cloneable, by the way, when you call "clone()" on it you'll get a "CloneNotSupportedException" exception, so remember your try/catch blocks!

Example: Using Java's cloneable to produce shallow copies of objects:

// Here's how to do a shallow copy:

```java
class ShallowCopyExample implements cloneable{

    // class contents here! We don't care about them for this example, though.  Only
    // overriding the clone() method from Object to insert a try/catch block...

    public ShallowCopyExample clone( ){
        try{
            return (ShallowCopyExample) super.clone( );   // Note the cast!
        }
        catch(CloneNotSupportedException e){
            return null;  // shouldn't happen, but you can check for null easily enough.
        }
    }
}
```

// And now for an example of how to call the clone() method:

ShallowCopyExample sampleShallowCopy = new ShallowCopyExample();

someMethod(sampleShallowCopy.clone());   *// Passing the clone, i.e. a copy.*

// that's all there is to it, IF you're satisfied with a shallow copy.

But wait; what if you want to do a deep copy? A deep copy is one in which even the reference variables' *contents* in your object are copied to new memory locations. To do this, you have to do a little more work. The first step is the same as with a shallow copy. You have to implement cloneable. But *then*, you have to create your *own* clone() method, one that does a deep copy. In order to do *this*, you have to have included some sort of "set" method for forcing a value into each of your reference variables. For example, if you've got a string variable "firstName", you would have to provide a method like "setFirstNameValue(String firstName)" in your object. Then, you would override Object's "clone()" method and set your version up to return the right object type and perform a deep copy. Here's a really small example (next page):

Example: Using cloneable to do a deep copy of an object:

class DeepCopyExample implements cloneable{

   // We can safely ignore most of the class, but let's assume the following Strings are
   // defined:

   Protected String firstName = "Phil";
   Protected String lastName = "Perry";

   // Here's a constructor that doesn't do much:
   DeepCopyExample(){

   }

   // We have to define a "setter" for our reference variables, so we can clobber them
   // if we want... Some reference variables may themselves be clonable, and you'll be
   // able to use clone() to copy those. Strings are not. Basically, for convenience, set
   // all the reference variables up in this function for deep copy purposes. Note that
   // this also means you don't have to make anything else public, only the methods.

   public setFirstName(String firstNameIn){
      firstName = new String(firstNameIn);
   }

   public setLastName(String lastNameIn){
      lastName = new String(lastNameIn);
   }

   // So, now, we do our deep copy version of clone( ):

   public DeepCopyExample clone( ){

      // You have to call the regular clone first, to do a shallow copy:
      DeepCopyExample deepCopy = (DeepCopyExample) super.clone( );   // casting!

      // At this point, deepCopy only contains a shallow copy of the object... So,
      // we clobber its reference variables so they point at new copies of the old ones,
      // using our set methods. The old copy's reference variables will still
      // point at the old data, and the new copy's reference variables will point at the
      // new copy of the data, elsewhere in memory.

      deepCopy.setFirstName(firstName);
      deepCopy.setLastName(lastName);

      // Now, return the cloned object.
      return(deepCopy);

   }

}

// Example -- using the deep copy clone:

DeepCopyExample sampleDeepCopy = new DeepCopyExample();

someMethod(sampleDeepCopy.clone());   // Passing the clone, i.e. a copy.

   How you write your deep copy will depend on how complicated the objects in your class are and how ambitious you are about copying them. Also, you'll have to ask yourself whether you really NEED a deep copy in the first place; it might be a whole lot easier just to keep in mind that you're working with reference variables and try not to break anything while you're calling methods (i.e. just be careful!).

   But you WILL sooner or later find out you have to write a deep copy, and now, you know how to do it. I had to Google all over the place to get the skinny on this, so hopefully I've saved you some time.

One Last Note on Objects:

Remember that interfaces and abstract base classes aren't mutually exclusive. You can use an interface to define all your public method signatures, and an abstract base class to provide a reference implementation (you should use variables of the abstract class type to hold child class objects because they'll have the benefit of its protected members, which won't be visible to a variable based on an interface).

When it comes to graphical user interfaces, I generally don't worry about creating interfaces or abstract base classes for my visually oriented objects because they're usually "one-offs" (created only once, for some specific purpose like data entry). Besides, I generate my user interfaces using NetBeans, I never write them by hand. I save a lot of time by restricting my coding to actual data-oriented classes, letting my tools handle as much of the plumbing as possible.

Remember to avoid private methods and variables, because they're not friendly towards your coworkers. Try to stick to protected and public; let your public methods follow a published interface your coworkers know about.

In case things still aren't 100% clear, you can go to Java.sun.com and look for the official Sun Java tutorial, which has a useful Objects section. It's good material and may help. You can find it here:

http://java.sun.com/docs/books/tutorial/java/concepts/index.html

Chapter 5: Java Exception Handling

If you've seen an earlier version of this book, you'll know that previously, I added exception handling to a small section of Chapter 3. Later, I expanded it to fill Chapter 4, with Chapter 5 being an introduction to OOP. Well, I've updated this book again, with a bit more information and an improved layout; for example, I moved the OOP chapter before this one so I could talk to you about extending the Exception object to make custom Exceptions of your own (this can be very useful).

This chapter is about handling exceptions, things that go wrong at runtime and could crash your program. By "catching" exceptions and dealing with their causes, we can avoid program crashes and help our users work around whatever problems are causing trouble. In other words, we can make our software much more robust. Exceptions are a very important, central part of Java programming.

Early on, when I was still learning, the first approach I took to handling exceptions was meant to streamline things, i.e. make it easier to help the user to adjust whatever he was doing. I was doing a solo project, and I set things up so that every exception would be caught and handled when it occurred. My classes would set a status variable ("OK" or "ERROR:" with a detailed guess as to what had gone wrong) and error messages would be passed back to the user. This worked out pretty well for me, but I still wasn't satisfied with it, so I spent some time trying to come up with a better approach.

The first thing I did was to search the web for best practices relating to exception handling. Unfortunately, nobody could seem to agree on any. There were numerous different opinions about what the best practices for Java exceptions actually *were*, with most people divided into two camps. The first camp followed the official Sun Microsystems standard, which used "checked exceptions" for all predictable error conditions and "unchecked exceptions" for serious malfunctions you couldn't recover from (like out of memory errors). The other camp absolutely hated checked exceptions, and thought everything should be done with unchecked exceptions and custom exceptions derived from them. Both groups seemed very knowledgeable, but I noticed that many of the guys who were against checked exceptions had formerly been C++ programmers. One of them mentioned that C++ doesn't even have checked exceptions. I decided that they were suffering from platform bias, like the old-timers who would joke that "you can program Fortran in any language". I decided to lean towards the Sun standard.

I read forum posts all day, followed bitter arguments, read through countless diatribes, and printed out a few tutorials, particularly sections of the Sun Java Tutorial. By the time I was done, I had a nice, mainstream, middle of the road approach figured out that used a combination of checked exceptions and unchecked exceptions.

The first part of this chapter will explain all the standard "nuts and bolts" of exception handling (along with some suggestions about things that have worked for me). The middle part will explain the standard approach to exception handling (the one used by many programmers); I'll explain why I think it causes trouble in practice. The last part of this chapter will explain the approach I've been using, which I think is simpler and easier to use than the standard one.

An Introduction to Java Exceptions:

Many of the things you can do with Java can fail at runtime. For example, you could try to open a file that doesn't exist, attempt to read from a database connection that had been closed due to network problems, or fail to read an XML file the user had somehow corrupted. In cases like these, your code will fail because of conditions outside of your control. Back in the bad old days, your program would just crash and "dump core" (save a binary file containing a representation of the last state the program was in). If you really blew it, you could crash the operating system or cause the system to hang. With modern languages like Java, you can usually "catch" the error and handle it elegantly.

Chapter 5: Exception Handling

In a broad sense, there are two kinds of Java exceptions: checked exceptions, and unchecked exceptions. You can break unchecked exceptions down further into runtime exceptions and errors.

Most problems that occur due to a user error (like a bad database password or filename) will cause checked exceptions to be thrown. In cases like these, you should catch the error, interpret its cause, and prompt the user to correct it.

Programming errors (like trying to access an uninitialized object in your code) will throw unchecked exceptions. The user usually won't be able to do anything about these, so it's pointless to let him see them; it's better to catch the exception, interpret it if possible, and show the user a generic explanation (like "Failed to connect; is the network down?") so they'll call tech support.

Finally, if something terrible happens (like an important subsystem crashing just as your program is accessing it), your code will generate an error. The user will generally be able to do nothing about errors; again, it's better to show them a generic explanation (i.e. "This computer appears to be crashing; exiting program") and shut your program down. With luck, they'll call tech support.

All Java exceptions are derived from java.lang.Exception. Unchecked exceptions derive from either java.lang.RuntimeException or java.lang.Error (which both derive from Exception).

Handling Exceptions Using Try/Catch Blocks:

In order to handle exceptions, you need to wrap any code that might experience a failure in a "try" block. After this block, you'll create a set of "catch" blocks to handle the exceptions you're expecting to see. After your last catch block, you'll create a "finally" block for cleanup.

In your catch blocks, you can choose from four possible responses to an exception: you can attempt to recover from it, perhaps repeating the task a set number of times; you can pass it up to the calling code and let another programmer choose what to do about it; you can trap it, and warn the user with a message; or you can log it out to an error file. You can also combine more than one of these approaches; many people always log exceptions, no matter what they do with them.

In your finally block, you should close out any objects you're using and set their variables to null, so they're ready to be garbage collected. Please look over the following *highly simplified* syntax and example:

Syntax of Try/Catch Error Handling Code:

try{

    // Code that might cause an Exception to be thrown.

}
catch(Exception e){

    // Code that handles the Exception (the "Exception Handler").
    // Note that I'm simplifying here by handling the most generic
    // possible Exception. In "real life" you'd be catching one of
    // several checked exceptions and doing something different for
    // each type.

}
finally{

    // Code that will always be run after the try/catch block. You should do
    // cleanup here. This is optional; to save space, I won't always put it
    // in my examples. But in "real life" you should ALWAYS do cleanup
    // in a finally block, to ensure that all your objects are garbage collected
    // and whatnot. HINT: always make sure an object isn't null with an
    // "if(someObject != null)" BEFORE you try to call any methods like

```
    // "close()".  You don't want to throw null pointer exceptions in
    // finally.
}
```

Here's a simple example:

```
try {
    String myString;
    // The following throws an exception because you can't call length() on
    // an uninitialized String (a String that's still null):
    if(myString.length() <= 0) myString = "empty";
}
catch(NullPointerException e){
    // NOTE: a null pointer exception is a type of runtime exception.
}
finally{
    // You'd clean up your objects here.
    myString = null;
}
```

Note that although finally is technically optional, you should ALWAYS use a finally block for cleanup.

The important thing about finally is that it ALWAYS runs, no matter what happens. Even if you have a "return" from your method or throw an exception back up to the calling code, the finally block will run FIRST. By putting your cleanup code here, you don't have to worry about missing it somehow, or duplicating it to cover all the ways in which you return from a method.

Specific Types of Exceptions You Can Catch:

Exceptions come in a variety of types; the Exception object has been extended to many child classes, each of which represents a specific type of problem like SQLException or IOException. Since they are all derived from Exception, of course this means that an Exception object can hold any type of Exception object that can be thrown.

You can use as many catch statements as you want in your try/catch blocks; if there's an exception, your program will move to the first "catch" block that matches it. If you have several catch blocks for specific exceptions, and an unexpected exception type is encountered, it won't match any of the catch blocks and it'll propagate up to the calling code. If the calling code doesn't handle it, it'll continue to propagate upward until it's either caught or crashes the program. This deserves some explanation, so let's digress a little.

When an Exception is thrown, the Java runtime first looks for a handler for that type of exception in the current method. If it doesn't find one, it throws the Exception up to the method that called the current method and looks for a handler there. If it doesn't find a handler there, it throws the Exception up to the next method, and the next, and so on until it either gets handled or causes the program to crash and display a stack trace (a list of all the methods the Exception travelled through before the crash).

NOTE: an Exception handler defined to catch a specific type of Exception can also catch any Exception derived from it. For example, the generic Exception can also catch SQLException.

Basically, if you've got three methods that have called each other in turn, and each is running its code in a try/catch block, and the innermost method throws an Exception, the Java runtime will check each method in turn, from the innermost outward, until it finds an Exception handler that can accept the Exception. Like a bubble moving up through water, the Exception will continue to be propagated upward until something stops it or it reaches the top level. At that point, it'll be displayed to the user in the Java console, who will be startled and annoyed by it, so try not to let that happen.

Each method you write has a simple choice to make with respect to Exceptions: handle the Exception, or pass it on upwards.

Let's do an example. Let's say you're going to call a method that can throw any of several possible exceptions. You want to handle all of these, but propagate other exceptions upward to the calling code. Take a look at the following sample code; in it, assume I'm trying to use a FileWriter to write out to a file (although I'm omitting the code, because it's irrelevant here), and I'm worried about getting an IOException while using the write() method, or a NullPointerException with another object I'm using to generate output. This try/catch block will let me deal with either of them:

Example: a Try/Catch Block Catching Two Types of Exceptions:

```
try{
    // Code that might throw an IOException.
}
catch(IOException ioe){
    // deal with it in some way
}
catch(NullPointerException npe){
    // deal with it in some way
}
finally{
    // Cleanup
}
```

Please remember that an exception handler can handle the exception it was declared for, as well as any exceptions that are derived from that exception. What this means is that if one exception is derived from another, you should place the derived exception's handler FIRST; otherwise, the more generic handler will devour all exceptions of both types.

In my opinion, you will generally not want to catch the generic Exception in any of the classes or methods where you're doing the actual work of your software, but you should catch it at the top level, in your "main()" method or (if you're writing GUI software) in your user interface code. This is because you don't EVER want to let your programs crash in front of a user. When a user sees a stack trace, the first thing that occurs to him is "this software is buggy and untrustworthy". Your goal as a programmer should be to handle Exceptions so this doesn't happen.

In other words, if none of your exception handlers matches an exception, wait until the last possible moment and catch the generic exception, converting it to a readable error for the user. The best place to do this is probably at the GUI level, where you can show the user a graphical response.

Passing Exceptions Back to Calling Code:

We've been talking about passing Exceptions back up to the calling code. In this section, let's talk about what you have to do to make this possible. In order to allow your methods to throw Exceptions back up to the calling code, all you have to do is change your method declaration so it includes the "throws" keyword followed by a list of possible exceptions you'll throw. Separate the list of Exceptions with commas. Here's the syntax, and an example:

Syntax for writing a method that can pass exceptions back up to calling code:

`access modifier` `return type` `method name` `(parameter list)` **throws**
   `exception-type1`, `exception-type2`, ... `exception-typeN` {

   // code here

}

// Example:

public String getResponse(String someSQLQuery) throws SQLException{

   // Your code here -- you might even have a try/catch in here, handling other
   // exceptions besides SQLException. As long as you don't have a catch for
   // SQLException, the uncaught exception will be thrown back to the calling
   // code. It'll basically fall through the function and keep going back to the
   // code that called the function. But in this case, <u>don't catch the general</u>
   // <u>exception or you'll never throw your SQLException!</u>

}

What you'll generally want to put in a throws clause is exception types that require some sort of corrective action on the part of the user, or at least the calling code. For example, if you encounter an SQLException, propagate it upwards using the throws keyword. The calling code can ask the user for a new password (or an account with more privileges) and try again.

You don't need to supply a throws clause for any non-checked Exceptions. As we discussed earlier, these relate to programmer errors or major system problems, so there's often nothing you or your user can do about them anyway. If you can reasonably react to them in your code, you can catch them and deal with them, but in general, you should probably let them propagate all the way up to the user interface level, catch them with a generic Exception so the program doesn't crash, and formulate some kind of polite error message so the user doesn't panic.

Throwing Your Own Exceptions:

Another thing Java lets you do is throw your own Exceptions at will. Let's say something happens in your code, something that you consider an error but which by itself won't cause an Exception to be thrown. You can manually create an Exception, forcing your program to deal with the situation just as if a normal Exception had been thrown. Here's the syntax to create and throw an Exception at runtime:

Syntax For Throwing Your Own Exceptions:

throw (new `exception type` ("`exception error message`"));

// For example:

throw (new RuntimeException("The resource you are looking for cannot be found."));

// This can be really, really useful.

Now that we're done with the basics, let's look at how Exceptions are used in practice. First, we'll look at the mainstream approach, and then we'll look at a simplified approach I've been using.

The Mainstream Java Approach to Exceptions:

For any given method that might encounter an Exception, if the Exception is something you can recover from right there without asking the user to do anything, go ahead and write a catch block for it that takes care of the problem. Of course this almost never happens. Almost all errors are USER errors.

For any Exception that needs input from the user or from the calling code, like SQLException (where you usually need to get a better password or an account with more privileges), you should use "throws" and pass the Exception up towards the calling code so your fellow programmers can decide how to respond to it. For Exceptions you can't do anything about, like RuntimeExceptions or system Errors, you should also pass the Exception up towards the calling code and let the programmer handle it as he wishes.

NOTE: This approach was designed by people who spent most of their time writing Java libraries, which are primarily used by programmers. If you're writing a low-level library, of *course* you want to propagate exceptions upward because you don't know how other programmers are going to use the library; you don't want to second guess them. For example, many Java gurus admonish us never to catch the generic Exception because it hides detail.

The problem with this is, most of us "mere mortal" Java programmers work on applications, not libraries, and it is fairly important for us to avoid startling our users. For example, if you're writing a user interface, you MUST catch the generic Exception and convert it to some kind of useful message for the user (and tech support). Remember: to a user, a stack trace is proof your program sucks. You want to look incompetent and unreliable and get taken off your projects in double-quick time? It's easy. Let your users see a stack trace. All it takes is one, and everyone will be talking about how buggy your code is. Let's look at some other ways in which the standard approach falls down in user-facing projects.

Why the Standard Approach Isn't So Hot If You're An Applications Programmer:

Imagine you're working on a project. You're responsible for a batch of back-end code that handles a database connection, and you've got a couple dozen methods, some of which are public and will be used by other programmers in your department. As in most I.T. departments, some percentage of your coworkers aren't very good at programming and of course, they will be using your code in their work.

You've got a number of methods that can fail at runtime in unpredictable ways. For example, you might see a SQLException, which usually relates to a bad password or lack of privileges. This exception should result in a message for the user, so you propagate it upward, along with a bunch of other possible exceptions that might be thrown (your methods have long "throws" clauses). Maybe sometimes a network problem causes a RuntimeException or an Error, but you always propagate those upward because you can't do anything about them. In other words, you're following the standard approach. How can this cause you problems?

For one thing, other programmers may not be thrilled at having to write five or six catch blocks every time they call your code. Certain programmers are going to be tempted to cut corners, catch Exception, and throw a stack trace at the users. This causes the users to become annoyed and take it out on the tech support dweebs, who will complain bitterly to their managers. They in turn will complain to your manager. He will ask you why your code is causing all these problems. Anything you say will sound like an excuse. Managers don't know anything about exception handling.

Another thing to consider: If you throw a bunch of possible Exceptions and Errors upwards, your fellow programmers will deal with them in completely unpredictable ways. Some might do the right thing with them, and write good, solid code. Others might not deal with them at all, letting them propagate all the way to the user. Saying this is "their fault" isn't going to cut it with your boss, who has no way of evaluating who is at fault. He may believe you, or the other guy. It's a coin toss.

My point is that if you just "program by contract" and assume your butt is covered, you're probably going to be in for a big, nasty surprise. Someone's going to drop the ball, and ultimately your code's going to look buggy. The traditional approach to Exception handling requires a LOT of trust in your fellow programmers. I don't like that. I prefer to ensure that the future unravels in a predictable, deterministic way.

What I Like to Do Instead:

I've been thinking about how to simplify and streamline my exception handling for a couple of years now, ever since the first time I rewrote this chapter, and I think I've got the problem solved. The solution involves wrapping exceptions in a custom exception, and throwing the custom exception up to the calling code with a useful, descriptive, plain-English error message. In theory, if you do this consistently, the same exact way every single time, it practically idiot-proofs your code.

In the following example, let's pretend I'm writing a set of classes related to paper order forms a company's clients will be submitting. There are numerous types of order forms, but they're all based on a single abstract base class called OrderForm. I want them all to use the same type of exception when they report problems, for simplicity's sake. The first thing I'll do is create a new class called OrderFormException, which extends Exception:

An easy way to write a custom exception for use with a number of objects:

```
public class OrderFormException extends Exception{
    OrderForm(String errorMessage){
        super(errorMessage);
    }
    OrderForm(String errorMessage, Exception e){
        super(errorMessage, e);
    }
}
```

Note what I did there... My custom exception is really only a thin wrapper around Exception. All it does is force programmers to supply an errorMessage String, and allow them to supply a copy of the original Exception object in case they want to let their coworkers use stack traces.

Here's how this will be used: If I discover a user error at some point in my code, I'll use the first constructor to instantiate and throw one of these custom errors with a useful, English-language error message attached to it.

On the other hand, if I'm writing a try/catch block, for each type of exception I'm catching, I'll figure out the best, most descriptive error message I can. Then I'll use the second constructor to instantiate my custom exception, adding a reference to the exception I caught to it. This lets the programmers who use my objects get things like stack traces if they want them.

If, in my try/catch block, I see any RuntimeExceptions or Errors, I can trap those and wrap them in one of my custom exceptions as well, with a best guess as to what caused the problem.

The result will be that my OrderForm classes' methods will usually throw the same type of exception (unless it throws something serious, like an Error), which will always have a descriptive error message and possibly a source exception. This makes things pretty easy for any programmer who wants to use my code. All he has to do is catch the single Exception type I'm throwing and pass the descriptive message along to the user.

If your situation is too complicated to be handled with only one Exception type, you can create more than one custom Exception for your project and document what a programmer is supposed to do with the different Exceptions. The point is to lay out exactly what is supposed to happen when an exception is thrown. Don't just throw everything upwards without working on it. Simplify the situation and pass something useful upwards. Just remember that the point is to simplify things. Don't create so many custom Exceptions that you might as well have used the generic types instead.

Now let's look at some sample code showing how this might work in practice. The following examples use the previous OrderFormException object for their exception handling needs:

Chapter 5: Exception Handling

Example of using a custom exception to simplify error handling:

```
// Note that the following would go in your code, where you're handling exceptions.
// It doesn't go in the calling code; we'll look at that next.
String errorMessage = "";
try{
    if(clientName == null){
        throw(new OrderFormException("The client's name must be entered."));
    } else if(clientName.length() <= 0){
        throw(new OrderFormException("The client's name must be entered."));
    } // else if
    // More code, which may throw custom exceptions or regular ones.
}
catch(SQLException se){
    // Just for simplicity, for this example we'll assume it's a bad username/password.
    throw(new OrderFormException("Bad username/password.", se));
}
catch(RuntimeException re){
    // For this example, let's say that you've been getting a lot of RuntimeExceptions
    // thanks to a network issue that comes up periodically.
    throw(new OrderFormException("Network Issue: contact technical support.", re));
}
// Note that I'm NOT catching the general Exception here.  The point is to let your custom Exception
// propagate upwards until it's handled.
```

Note that when you're throwing an exception but you haven't caught one yet, you'll use the String-only constructor. When you're reacting to an exception you've caught, you'll use the String-and-exception constructor. Now let's see what the calling code looks like:

Calling code that must react to my custom exception:

```
try{
    // Some code that might trigger my custom exception.
}
catch(OrderFormException ofe){
    // Warn the user, etc.  We'll keep it simple for now and use standard output.
    System.out.println(ofe.getMessage());
}
```

I think that's not a bad way to do things. It's relatively idiot-proof, it can be pretty bulletproof if you're conscientious about handling every possible exception your code might encounter, and it gives you some control over the error messages that are shown to the user. You can make it pretty easy for the programmers using your code to provide user-friendly error messages and recover from errors.

Chapter 6: Working With the Filesystem

This chapter will be short and sweet. Java offers a generous selection of different types of file-related objects, and you'll want to check them out by looking over them in the API reference. I won't get into them all here, but you should at least know how to work with text files. This is something almost everybody does on a regular basis, and it's a good introduction to file I/O. It's also conveniently easy: there are only a few objects you'll need to know how to use.

Before we get started, in any code where you want to work with files, you'll need at least one or two of the following imports from the java.io package; please assume that these imports have already been made when you read the examples in this chapter:

Common File-Related Imports For Your Java Code:

```
import java.io.File;                // Almost always used.
import java.io.FileReader;          // Used for reading files.
import java.io.BufferedReader;      // Used for reading files.
import java.io.FileWriter;          // Used for writing files.
import java.io.BufferedWriter;      // Used for writing files.
import javax.swing.JFileChooser;    // Used for letting a user choose a file in a GUI.
```

Next, let's discuss something that both reading and writing text files have in common; both processes usually use a "File" object to specify the file they'll be manipulating. This object also gives you a lot of useful functionality. On the web, you'll see lots of sample code in which people skip using a File object, and just pass paths to files as Strings. Don't do this! Always try to start out with a File object. It's cleaner and you'll end up with better code in the long run. You set up a File object like this:

Syntax for Setting Up a File Object:

```
// Method one: an empty file, not pointing at any path yet:
File variable_name = new File ( );

// Example:
File localFile = new File ( );

// Method two: using a path, initialize the File object by opening an existing file:
File variable_name = new File (file_path_as_a_String);

// Note on paths: you'll want to set them up relative to your project directory,
// and use Java's built-in separator instead of an O/S specific character like "/".
// Try not to use absolute paths; relative paths are better. More on this later in the chapter.
// For now, just keep in mind that "using relative paths" == "portable code".
// For example, you should do something like this:
String variable_name = "subdirectory_name" + File.separator
                     + "subdirectory_name" + File.separator + "file_name";

// O/S Independent Example (path relative to project dir):
String localFilePath = "data" + File.separator + "someFile.txt";
File localFile = new File (localFilePath);
```

Once you've set up your file object, you can use it to see whether a file you're interested in is readable or writable, whether it exists, whether you have the right to create a file in a given directory, and so on. Let's look at the syntax for these tools, assuming we've created a file object called localFile, and that it's been fed a path to a file or directory. Many Java developers don't even use these tools, trying to make their code concise by cramming as much as possible into a single statement -- don't do that! Use these tools to make your code more robust (who cares if your code is a little longer?):

Syntax Examples for Working With File Objects:

```
// In the following, methods return "true" if they work, and "false" if
// they fail. If there's a security issue, like you don't have access, you'll
// get an exception. Remember your try/catch blocks! Assume we've
// declared and instantiated a File object called "localFile".

// Does your file/directory exist? It's nice to check before you try to do anything...
boolean exists = localFile.exists( );

// Is your file/directory readable? It's nice to check before reading...
boolean readable = localFile.canRead( );

// Is your file/directory writable? It's nice to check before writing...
boolean writable = localFile.canWrite( );

// Is it a directory? Check before trying to get a listing!
boolean isADir = localFile.isDirectory( );

// Is it a regular file? Check before trying to open it!
boolean isAFile = localFile.isFile( );

// If it is a directory, get a list of files in it:
File[ ] fileList = localFile.listFiles( );

// Even if your File is using a relative path in your project dir,
// you can get an absolute path for it, which will be O/S appropriate:
String absolutePath = localFile.getAbsolutePath();

// You can delete files too. Note that if your File is a directory, the directory MUST
// be empty or you won't be allowed to delete it. Be careful to capture exceptions!
boolean wasDeleted = localFile.delete( );

// You can create a whole new file if you want (if the file already exists, this method
// returns false; if you don't have access, you'll get an exception):
boolean fileCreated = localFile.createNewFile( );

// You can make a directory, too (true on success, false on failure):
boolean dirCreated = localFile.mkdir( );

// You can find out how big your file is in bytes (if it's a directory, you get nothing back,
// if you don't have read access, you get an exception):
long  fileSize = localFile.length( );

// Is it a hidden file? Note that under Unix-like systems, a hidden file is one whose
// name starts with a period, like this: ".something". Under Windows systems,
// a hidden file is one that has been marked in the filesystem as hidden. YOU
// don't have to worry about that; Java will figure it out for you. Just ask:
boolean hidden = localFile.isHidden( );

// If you want to know the actual filename (as opposed to the path) you can just use
// getName, which snips off the last name from the path for you:
String filename = localFile.getName( );

// And, finally, if you want to know the parent directory of your File's path, use the
// following (if you don't have a parent in the path, you'll get null back):
String parentDir = localFile.getParent( );
```

There are many other useful file and directory related methods in File, but these are the ones I personally use most often. Again, I keep saying you should check out the API reference, and this is yet another example of how useful you're going to find it.

At this stage, you know how to work with files at the File object level. Let's move on to the first common thing you'll want to do with a file, i.e. reading it in one line at a time and doing something with it.

Reading Files Sequentially with a BufferedReader:

This is the most common thing in the world: reading input data one line at a time from a file someone's emailed you and processing it in some way. You'll want to work with files one line at a time because you can't predict in advance how big they might be, and you don't want to end up accidentally gobbling up so much memory you noticeably slow the machine down. Here's how you do it, using sample code to show you the technique:

SAMPLE CODE: *How to read a text file one line at a time:*

```
// First you're going to want to declare the following variables:
String currentFilePath = "data" + File.separator + "test.txt";   // relative path!
File inputFile;
FileReader inputFileReader;
BufferedReader inputFileData;
String currentLine;

// These variables are declared more or less in the order in which you're going to
// use them.  Basically, you'll create a File object for your target file, then you'll pass
// that to a FileReader, then pass THAT to a BufferedReader.  These objects act like
// layers through which your data passes; the BufferedReader should be thought of
// as the TOP layer, the one that gives you a nice, streamlined interface for interacting
// with your file.  Let's move along...

// Now, we'll instantiate the objects (do this in a try/catch block!!!):
try {
    inputFile = new File(currentFilePath);
    inputFileReader = new FileReader(inputFile);
    inputFileData = new BufferedReader(inputFileReader);

    // Ok, at this point, you have a BufferedReader ready to go.  If you're working
    // with text, you'll want to read in one line (logical record) at a time; Java will
    // consider a line to be a set of text terminated with a line termination character.
    // On unix systems, this will generally be a line feed (\n). On Windows systems
    // this will be a carriage return AND a line feed (\r\n). On Macs (just to be contrary?),
    // Apple just uses an \r.  Which character you get depends on which system the
    // file was originally CREATED on.  Just keep this in mind -- Java will read your
    // line in the same way either way, so it shouldn't affect your programming (the
    // JRE knows which system it's running on).  But if you look at your file in a low-
    // level editor like VI, you'll see different characters in some files. FYI.

    // First thing's first: read an initial line just to get things going. readLine() gets
    // everything up to (but not including) the end-line character(s).
    currentLine = inputFileData.readLine();

    // Now start a while loop.  You want to continue to read data until there's no
    // data left. Note: As each record comes in, you'll want to do something to
    // it. Maybe you're reading records in and storing them in a database. Maybe
    // you're scrolling them on the screen. Whatever.  You get the idea.

    while( currentLine != null) {
```

```java
            // Do something with the data here. When you're done, read the next line in.
            currentLine = inputFileData.readLine();
        }
        // Now we test inputFileData and inputFileReader for null (always a good
        // idea) and close them. This could throw an IOException.
        if(inputFileData != null){
            inputFileData.close();
        }
        if(inputFileReader != null){
            inputFileReader.close();
        }
    }
    catch(IOException ioe){
        // Do something appropriate here to let your user know things are bollixed up.
    }
    finally{
        // Null out your objects here for cleanup.
        inputFileData = null;
        inputFileReader = null;
        inputFile = null;
    }
```

So, that's pretty much it as far as reading a file in a line at a time goes. It's pretty easy, requires very little code, and because we're only looking at one line at a time, takes up almost no memory at all. Note that if you want to go back to the beginning of the file, you would issue the BufferedReader's "**reset( )**" method call.

ON CODE PORTABILITY:

Note how I used File.separator instead of a hard-coded string like "/". The reason for this is simple: different operating systems use different characters as separators in the path to your file. It behooves you to let the JVM select the appropriate one for your current operating system. For example, Windows uses "\" while Linux and Mac OS/X both use "/". Let the JVM handle it! It makes your code MUCH easier to port.

Here's something else you'll want to be aware of. Notice that I used a relative path when I specified where my file was. Relative paths always start in your program's installation directory (wherever you'll be running your main program from). Here, I'm assuming the existence of a subdirectory called "data" and in that subdirectory, an input file called "test.txt". This is the best approach if you want your code to be cross-platform! **You want to avoid absolute paths whenever possible.** The reason for this is very simple. Every operating system out there, and even different distributions of Linux, have different directory structures. Is a Linux user's directory under /home? Or did the sysadmin put it somewhere else? If your program is being ported to a Windows machine, did the user install his system to the C:\ drive or the D:\ drive? Or E:\? Or is he running your code from a network drive like "\\myStuff"? You can call methods that will fetch you the current working directory path and build an absolute path from there, but why bother? Just use relative paths, keep your data in your own directory, and stop worrying about the whole thing.

Writing Data Out to a File Using BufferedWriter:

This works almost exactly like reading data using a BufferedReader, only this time we'll be writing data OUT a line at a time. As far as line terminators go, I usually absent-mindedly use "\n" (the unix approach) and don't worry about Microsoft's "\r\n" or Apple's "\r". Most word processors and text editors will be able to recognize this approach, so you won't lose anything by using it, and your output files will look the same no matter what platform they were created on. However, if you want to output newlines in an O/S specific way determined by the system the user's working with, BufferedWriter offers a method that will give you an OS-specific line termination character, "**newLine( )**". I'll use it in my example.

As before, I'll demonstrate using working source code:

SAMPLE CODE: Writing data out to a file, line by line.

```
String currentFilePath = "data" + File.separator + "test.txt";    // relative path!
File outputFile;
FileWriter outputFileWriter;
BufferedWriter outputFileBufferedWriter;

try{

    outputFile = new File(currentFilePath);
    outputFileWriter = new FileWriter(outputFile);
    outputFileBufferedWriter = new BufferedWriter(outputFileWriter);

    // NOTE: I'm creating a kind of hokey example with this simple array of Strings.
    // In "real life" you'll have some way of generating outputs for your file.  If you're
    // logging database errors, for example, you'll open your BufferedWriter and keep
    // it available during your database session, writing your errors out as you go.

    // HOKEY ARRAY OF STRINGS JUST FOR THIS EXAMPLE:
    String [ ] myHokeyArray = { "First String", "Second String", "Third String" };

    // Now, you'll generally loop over your output data, or you'll be writing out
    // database errors on the fly, but let's do a for loop and spit out our three Strings:

    for(i = 0;  i < 3; i++){
        outputFileBufferedWriter.write(myHokeyArray[i]);
        outputFileBufferedWriter.newLine( );
    }

    // Now we check each writer for null and close it. This may throw an IOException.
    // Closing an already-closed writer has no effect.

    if(outputFileBufferedWriter != null){
        outputFileBufferedWriter.close( );
    }


    if(outputFileWriter != null){
        outputFileWriter.close( );
    }

}
catch(IOException ioe){
    // Here you'd do something sensible and useful to your users, letting them
    // know an error has taken place.
}
finally{
```

```
    // Now null out the objects.
    outputFileBufferedWriter = null;
    outputFileWriter = null;
    outputFile = null;
}
```

That's all there is to writing data out to a file. It's just as easy as reading data in, and doesn't take a whole lot of code.

While we're on the topic of writing data out to a file, here's some free advice: As you get more experienced, you'll find yourself working with more complicated projects. You may find yourself writing out XML files, or PDF files, or some other file format that's even more complicated. Before you go nuts trying to roll your own classes to perform this work, SEARCH THE WEB. It's highly likely someone else has already done it for you, and you can use their beautiful open-source library to do it without having to write it yourself. For example, if you want to write PDFs, check out the wonderful PDF library "**iText**" at http://www.lowagie.com/iText/. I've used this at work, and it produces marvellous PDF output. Most of the complicated things you might have to do in a business setting have already been done by someone else, and it pays to look around a little before you spin your wheels. FYI.

One More Neat Trick Before I go:

Before I wrap up this chapter on the filesystem, I'd like to share one more useful tip. As you start building your GUIs and writing user interface code, sooner or later you're going to come to a point where you're going to have to pop up some kind of interface to let your user select a file. You don't have to build this interface yourself; Java's standard library includes the class JFileChooser, which automatically pops up a beautiful, O/S friendly file selection interface and hands you back an absolute path to whatever file the user has selected. Here's how to use it:

NEAT TRICK: Using JFileChooser to Let Users Select Files:

```
// Whenever you have to let users select a file or directory, use the object
// "javax.swing.jFileChooser". All you have to do when a user wants to open a file is the
// following:

// Import the following at the top of your file, for convenience.
import javax.swing.JFileChooser;

// Somewhere convenient, declare a String to hold the currently selected directory
// (using "." means "the program's current directory"):
String currentDirectory = ".";

// You'll want to also create a String to hold the path of the file the user selects.
String currentFilePath;

// In your code, where the user has actually requested the opening of a file, do this:
JFileChooser chooser = new JFileChooser(currentDirectory);

// Next, after you instantiate your chooser, you'll want to set what the user can select,
// using one of the following commands (pick the one that applies to your application).
// FILES_ONLY is the default option;
chooser.setFileSelectionMode(JFileChooser.DIRECTORIES_ONLY);
chooser.setFileSelectionMode(JFileChooser.FILES_AND_DIRECTORIES);
chooser.setFileSelectionMode(JFileChooser.FILES_ONLY);

// We show a file open dialog, giving this current window as its parent
// object. returnVal indicates what the user clicked -- ok or cancel.
int returnVal = chooser.showOpenDialog(this);
```

```
// If the user clicked "OK", returnVal will equal the constant
// JFileChooser.APPROVE_OPTION.
// we'll also get the absolute path to the user's selected file.
if(returnVal == JFileChooser.APPROVE_OPTION) {
    currentFilePath = chooser.getSelectedFile().getAbsolutePath();
}
// The following lets us "remember" which directory the user was looking at.
// This is convenient if you don't want to make the poor user browse to
// the directory each and every time he opens a file.
currentDirectory = chooser.getCurrentDirectory().toString();
```

Note that because the file chooser generates a platform-specific path when the user selects a file or directory, you won't have to tailor any of your code for the user's specific operating system. This is one of the only situations in which absolute paths don't cause you platform-specific headaches. If you want to do any processing on the path, you should use it to instantiate a File object, then use the methods in File to pull out parts of the path. If you make the mistake of processing the path like a String, you'll end up with code that isn't cross-platform. Note that if all you're doing is using the path to open a file, you don't have to parse it at all, so it won't matter which platform the path was generated on.

A Suggestion for Additional Study:

You won't be doing this too often, but there may come a time at which you want to read files in random access mode, i.e. jumping around a file to specific positions, measured in bytes from the beginning of the file.

Alternatively, you may find you need to read and write binary files (for example, if you've got to store word-processor documents in a database, and need to be able to read them in and write them out without corrupting them).

For cases like these, Java offers a "**RandomAccessFile**" object. Random access files tie into file structures, but this sort of thing is outside the scope of my small book. If you find yourself in need, you should check the API reference and google for some online tutorials about "file structures" and "file processing" to get started.

Chapter 7: Using JDBC to Interact With Databases:

Every programmer in a corporate or government environment needs to know how to query and update a database. It's not a terribly complicated topic in terms of the code you'll have to write, but this is deceptive. All the real complexity comes from designing the queries and update statements in SQL, so you'll want to get yourself a good book on the subject and read it. Alternately, you can find many good online tutorials on the subject. Once you're ready, this chapter will give you the Java part of the picture.

Before we begin, I'd like to share some tips on how to get Apache Derby running on your desktop machine. Derby is a totally free, fully relational embedded database (i.e. a database you can build right into the software you write). I think it's about the coolest thing since sliced bread, so you really MUST give it a try. Why use flat files for data storage when you can build a proper database schema and interact with your data using SQL?

Setting Up Apache Derby And Creating Your First Empty Database:

The first thing you'll need to do is actually *get* Derby. Look for it here: http://db.apache.org/derby/. The download is a zip file which contains an entire Derby directory, ready to go. Just unzip it somewhere convenient, like your home directory. Next, in the directory where you installed Derby, find the "lib" subdirectory. We don't want to bother starting up a whole Derby server; we just want to run it in embedded mode. So what we're going to do is grab derby.jar and derbytools.jar from the "lib" directory of the Derby installation directory, copy them to a "Derby" directory somewhere convenient, and delete the Derby installation directory. Go ahead and do this.

Now, derbytools.jar contains a wonderful program called "IJ". You can use this program to create new databases, and work with existing databases using SQL. It frees you from having to use a graphical tool, so it's very useful. Let's open up a command line window and go to the "Derby" directory you just created (you can name it whatever you want, but "Derby" is self-documenting). Then, first issue this command to add derby.jar and derbytools.jar to your CLASSPATH:

export CLASSPATH=$CLASSPATH:./derby.jar:./derbytools.jar   < On Linux

export CLASSPATH=%CLASSPATH%;.\derby.jar;.\derbytools.jar   < Should work on Windows

Then, issue this command to start up IJ:

java org.apache.derby.tools.ij

You should get an IJ prompt, like this:

ij version 10.8

ij>

To create a new database, all you have to do is connect to it using the right kind of JDBC URL. Let's create a database named "testDerby". The command looks like this:

ij> connect 'jdbc:derby:testDerby;create=true';

After about a minute, you are returned to an IJ prompt, and you can exit by typing "exit" as shown:

ij> exit;

Check the directory, and you should see a brand-new Apache Derby database waiting for you. Derby databases are completely self-contained within a single directory. In this case, we got a directory called "testDerby". We can now copy this directory wherever we want to use it. Generally we'll want to put it in the working directory of any software we want to access it with. For NetBeans projects, we'll want to create two copies of our Derby directory. The first one goes in the root directory of our NetBeans project, so we can access the database while debugging (NetBeans uses this directory as the project's working directory while you're running

Chapter 7: Using JDBC to Interact With Databases — Phil's Java Tutorial

the project in the IDE). The second one goes along with the project's jar file and lib directory when you roll it out to production. Put it in the same directory where you put the jar file, and you won't have any problems.

Connecting to Your Derby Database Using NetBeans, In Embedded Mode:

In NetBeans, click the "Window" menu, then "Services" to bring up the Services tab. This is where you'll find the "Databases" tool. Click the little arrow next to "Databases", expanding it. Now, right-click on "Drivers" and click "New Driver". A dialog window will appear. For "Driver Files" browse to your Derby directory and select "derby.jar". The driver class and name are automatically populated for you. Click "OK" to enable the driver. It'll appear in your drivers list.

To connect to your new database using NetBeans in embedded mode, just right-click the new embedded driver you've created, and click "Connect Using". This will bring up a dialog which will allow you to configure a new database connection. For the first text box, asking for the database's name, enter the full path to the database you just created. Note that the database URL is automatically prepared for you. Don't enter a userID or password, because we didn't create one. You don't have to; you can treat an embedded database as an unsecured data store if you want. An attacker would have to have access to a user's account to access it, so this is a reasonable approach. Now click "Test Connection" and make sure you can connect to the database. If you can't, double-check your path. Once you see "Connection Succeeded" you can click "finish" to wrap up (clicking "Next" only lets you see what the default schema for the database is – it's "App").

If everything went as planned, you should now see your database connection directly under the drivers list. It'll have a square yellowish icon, with a little arrow next to it. Click the arrow and look around. There's a folder for table definitions, one for view definitions, and one for stored procedures. Those are the three you're really interested in. If you right-click on the database connection, you can execute SQL commands in the command window that pops up. If you right-click on one of the three folders, you can create, delete, and otherwise work with tables, views, and stored procs. It's all pretty straightforward.

Incidentally, what I like to do is write a setup script in SQL that creates all my tables and sets up all my key relationships. This way, all I have to do is right click the connection, click "Execute Command", paste in my script and run it. I can create the same database as many times as I like without having to waste time with the mouse and the UI. It's a whole lot easier, believe me. A little time up front writing the script, and you never have to waste time again. Of course you can do the same thing with IJ!

Now that you've got Derby set up, and you've got the basic idea of how to work with it to create and edit databases, let's move on to actual JDBC, and talk about how you interact with a database using Java.

Configuring Your JDBC Database Drivers (Jar Files)

Let's assume you've chosen a database platform you want to work with (whether it's Derby, which we'll use for our examples, or Oracle, or something else) and now you want to do some database programming. The first thing you're going to need to do is get a copy of the JDBC database drivers from your vendor and set them up in NetBeans so you can integrate them into your project. Take these steps and you should be up and running:

1. Go to your database vendor's website (for example, www.apache.org for Derby) and hunt around until you've found their database drivers. These will almost certainly be in the form of a JAR file you can download. There may be more than one jar file; if so, keep them in the same directory.

   Remember, if you're using Derby, you won't get just the driver, you'll also get an install for a whole database you can run on your desktop, or you'll have received a whole database as part of a JDK/NetBeans bundle. Unzip the whole thing, grab your drivers (derby.jar and derbytools.jar) and delete it again. You just need the jar files, really, unless you want to run Derby as a server (which is possible!).

2. Save the JAR file or files you got from the vendor someplace convenient, like in a "DBDrivers" directory in your home directory on Linux, or in "C:\dbdrivers" on a Windows machine.

If you're using Derby, the driver you're looking for will be in the file "derby.jar" in the "lib" directory of your Derby install directory. Remember to grab "derbytools.jar" so you can run IJ.

If you're using Oracle, you've already got a copy of the drivers as a part of the client software everyone installs. In that case, look for the drivers in the "JDBC" directory in your Oracle install directory. Although, I like to get my drivers by download from Oracle and save them to their own directory; it simplifies the path to them. The path to the drivers in an Oracle install tends to be kind of on the long side.

3. In NetBeans, right-click your project, then click "Properties", and finally click "Libraries". On the right side of the properties window, click the "Add Jar/Folder" button. Browse to your database jar files, and add them to your project. Note that when you package your project for distribution, a copy of your driver JAR files will get packaged along with it in the "lib" directory, so don't worry about distributing them -- with a good IDE like NetBeans, this is done automatically for you.

You can also configure NetBeans to set up a centralized entry for your database jar files, to make it slightly easier to add them to multiple projects. Right-click your project, then click Properties, then Libraries, but this time click "Add Library" instead of "Add Jar/Folder". A library selection window will appear; click "Create". A window will appear letting you name your new library (give it a good, descriptive name). Then, a jar file selection window will appear. Click "Add Jar/Folder" as before, find your database jar files, and add them. Then click "OK"; the library will be created and added to the list of available libraries. It'll be pre-selected; click "Add Library" at the bottom of the window, and the new library will be added to your project. The new library will also be available whenever you want to add it to any other project.

How include your database libraries in your projects is up to you. It's mostly a matter of personal preference. Even if you're working on a team, you'll be working with your own copy of NetBeans and so will your teammates. The libraries will be included in your builds the same way no matter which approach you use, so either way is fine.

Now that you've got your drivers configured, you're ready to start actually using them. Let's move on to coding.

Opening a Database Connection In Your Code:

The very first thing your code will ALWAYS do is open up a database connection. In order to do this, you'll have to register a driver for your database vendor, then use that driver to return an open connection. There are two ways to do this; the first method uses DriverManager to register the driver, and the second uses Class.forName to register it (Class.forName is the newer approach). The difference really only affects a couple of lines of code, so it's not that big a deal; the approach you should choose depends on your database vendor and how you're interacting with their database. Once you've registered your driver, regardless of whether you used DriverManager or Class.forName, you'll need to use a static method in DriverManager to obtain a Connection object; the Connection object is what you use to actually access the database.

For example, if you're using an older version of Oracle's development tools (like the JDeveloper that came with the original 10G Developer Suite), or you're deploying your software to users who are using the 10G Oracle client software, all of these tools use an Oracle-provided JDK 1.4.2, so you have to use DriverManager. Even if you download a brand-new JDeveloper, if you're writing servlets or anything else that will be posted to a 10G application server, you're STILL stuck with 1.4.2 because that's the version of the JVM the app server will be running. It won't be able to handle code compiled with newer versions of Java. If you're in an Oracle shop, it's safer to use the DriverManager approach and the JDK Oracle has provided.

On the other hand, if you're not in an Oracle shop and you're using NetBeans or Eclipse and a current JDK, then you can use the newer approach with Class.forName. Almost all the other database vendors out there are agnostic towards Java; they don't provide their own proprietary JDK, so if you want to use Java to connect to them, you can choose whatever JDK you want. They'll provide you a driver as a jar file, and since Java is backwards compatible, the driver will usually work with whatever Java you happen to be running. Naturally I really prefer this situation. I think it's a lot more flexible.

As an aside, I'm not trying to beat up Oracle here. I think the reason Oracle has maintained their own version of Java for so long must be that since they use Java internally in their software, they're cautious about leaving its development up to another company. In other words, they can't afford for changes in Java to break their software, so they maintain their own in-house version. I understand, and I even sympathize, but I personally wouldn't have chosen that approach.

Here are two sets of sample code for you to look at; the first one assumes you're connecting to an Oracle database, and the second one assumes you're using Apache Derby, the embedded Java database the Apache Project distributes. The main differences between the two are in the database URL and in the method used to register the driver. I've shown them in bold text to draw attention to them; you'll notice that the rest of the code is nearly identical. After this first pair of samples, the rest of the examples in this chapter will use Derby (since it's free for download, you can get yourself a copy and play with it while you learn).

**SAMPLE CODE 1: *Connecting to a Database (using an Oracle-type connection string)*
*(Note: This is an old-fashioned method, you generally only need to use it with Oracle databases older than Oracle 11G, and maybe some other legacy systems, but keep it in mind!):***

```
// Remember to import java.sql.*; at the top of your class file.
import java.sql.*;

// The rest is assumed to be somewhere within your Java class, like in a method:
// Assume we have already received variables userID and userPassword from the user.

String databaseURL = "jdbc:oracle:thin:@192.168.0.1:1521:oracle";
Connection dbConnection;
try{

    // The following line  is Oracle-specific, when you're using the Oracle JVM;
    // The built-in Oracle JVM (for version 10G, at least)  is based on old Java,
    // JDK 1.4.2, so the driver uses the old method:
    DriverManager.registerDriver(new oracle.jdbc.driver.OracleDriver());
    dbConnection = DriverManager.getConnection(databaseURL,userID,userPassword);
    if(!(dbConnection.isClosed( ))){

        // here you would do something with your connection, like run a query.
        // we'll talk about that code in a minute.

    }

}
catch(SQLException sqle){

    // Here you would handle the SQL error, probably passing some sort of
    // meaningful message back to the user.  Generally it'll be something like
    // the database connection being lost during the query.  If your query is
    // just not returning any rows, that's not an error; that's a result.

}
finally {

    // Here you would clean up all your connections and null out your objects, like this:
    if(dbConnection != null){
        if(! (dbConnection.isClosed( ))){
            dbConnection.close( );
        }
        dbConnection = null;
    }
}
```

Sample Code 2: Using JDBC with Apache Derby
(This is how you connect to most databases; it's the "normal" approach):

```java
// Remember to import java.sql.*; at the top of your class file.
import java.sql.*;

// The rest is assumed to be somewhere within your Java class, like in a method:
// Assume we have already received variables userID and userPassword from the user.

String  databaseURL = "jdbc:derby:EXAMPLE";
Connection dbConnection;
try{
    // Here we open our database Connection. Note that the derby driver (derby.jar)
    // is a free download; you save it to your computer and add it to your project's
    // libraries in NetBeans; this makes it available in your code.
    Class.forName("org.apache.derby.jdbc.EmbeddedDriver");
     dbConnection = DriverManager.getConnection (databaseURL,
                                                  userID,
                                                  userPassword);
    if(!(dbConnection.isClosed( ))){
        // here you would do something with your connection, like run a query.
        // we'll talk about that code in a minute.
    }
}
catch(SQLException sqle){
    // Here you would handle the SQL error, probably passing some sort of
    // meaningful message back to the user.  Generally it'll be something like
    // the database connection being lost during the query.  If your query is
    // just not returning any rows, that's not an error; that's a result.
}
finally {
    // Here you would clean up all your connections and null out your objects, like this:
    if(dbConnection != null){
        if(! (dbConnection.isClosed( ))){
            dbConnection.close( );
        }
        dbConnection = null;
    }
}
```

A Little More About the Database URL:

The database URL, a String which you pass to the static getConnection method of the DriverManager class, will be in a format you'll find in your vendor's documentation. Somewhere in that documentation, you'll find a sample URL for your database. You'll modify this String to match your individual site's parameters, like IP address and port number (or in the case of Derby, the directory your embedded database is in).

For example, look at the Oracle URL. The first part, "jdbc:oracle:thin:" means you're using Oracle's "thin" driver, which is the best one to use in your applications. The "@" sign means, literally, "at" because the next part specifies the server you're using. Finally, the "192.168.0.1:1521:oracle" means you're connecting to the server with IP address 192.168.0.1, using port number 1521 (the standard Oracle port), and with the SID (the unique name you assign an Oracle database) "oracle". So, on Oracle systems, the part of the URL you'll be changing is the part AFTER the @ sign. Put in the appropriate IP address, port and SID and you'll be all set.

On Derby, things are much easier because an embedded database is usually entirely enclosed in a subdirectory of your software's working directory. The database URL, "*jdbc:derby:example*" just means we're using JDBC, with the derby driver, and targeting the database in the directory "example" in our project's main directory. Note that you can also use any valid relative path to your software's working directory. For example, if you want to put the Derby directory in a "resources" subdirectory, the relative path would be "resources/example" and the database URL would be "*jdbc:derby:resources/example*". It's easier to just keep the derby directory in the software's working directory, though. **Remember: in your code, always use relative paths, never use absolute paths.** You can't guarantee where a user will install your software, or whether he might do something weird with it like move it to a network share. If you use relative paths, and keep all your resources inside your project's working directory, you maximize your chances that your project will continue to work even if the user does something strange with it.

Once the Driver is Registered and You've Got a Connection Object:

Once the driver is registered, and you've called getConnection (passing it the database URL, the userID, and the user's password), it *should* return an open database connection object. But since you don't really know whether the connection is open yet, you'd better make sure it's open before you try to use it.

Just use an "if" statement and check the "isClosed()" method of the Connection object to see whether its state is open or not. If it turns out to be closed, you don't want to try and execute any queries because they'll just throw an exception and waste your time. Instead, warn the user that the database is closed and let it go at that.

Inside the "if" statement, after you've verified your Connection object is open, you'll actually work with the database.

NOTE: From here on in, all databases work in essentially the same way; the only differences you might notice are in extensions some vendors offer to their SQL, and in how well they support transactions. My examples will be Derby examples, because you can download it for free and play with it on your desktop, but aside from the differences already described, all the code works in exactly the same way for all databases.

Select Statements: Querying the Database:

The first thing I'm going to show you is how to do a query that fetches back data from your database without modifying anything. The example uses a Java PreparedStatement to run a SQL "select" query. PreparedStatements are called "parameterized statements" because you don't build your SQL statement by concatenating Strings. Instead, you use placeholders to represent variables, and in later statements, supply values for them.

This is MUCH SAFER than the older approach of concatenating Strings. In olden times, Java programmers used to use the Java "Statement" object to perform queries, supplying it with a SQL String they built by concatenating chunks of SQL with user-supplied variables. Hackers discovered that they could play jokes on people (or hack their servers) by supplying entire SQL statements instead of the String data the developers were expecting. As you might imagine, this did not amuse the developers, and a solution to this problem was provided in the form of parameterized statements. When you're using PreparedStatement instead of Statement, if someone tries to feed you some SQL instead of their address, it won't actually get executed. It'll probably throw an exception in fact.

This is a Very Good Thing, so use PreparedStatements anytime you're working with any user-supplied data! The *only* thing it's safe to use a plain Java Statement for is *static SQL that never changes* (i.e. something like "select * from fubar").

So, let's start with a simple query, reading some records from a database. The following example demonstrates how to run a plain, read-only query; instead of talking about it, it's easier to just show it to you:

SAMPLE CODE: Querying a Database Using a Parameterized Query:

```java
// Remember to import java.sql.*; at the top of your class file.
import java.sql.*;

// The rest is assumed to be somewhere within your Java class, like in a method:
// Assume we have already received variables userID and userPassword from the user.

// First, our database connection setup parameter:
String  databaseURL = "jdbc:derby:EXAMPLE";

// Next, Our database related objects:
Connection dbConnection;
PreparedStatement sqlStatement;
ResultSet queryResults;

// Two sample parameters for our example, and a string to fetch a phone # into:
String lookupName = "Joe Smith";
String lookupBirthday = "01-MAY-53";
String phoneNumber;

try{

    // Here we open our database Connection.
    Class.forName("org.apache.derby.jdbc.EmbeddedDriver");
    dbConnection = DriverManager.getConnection (databaseURL,
                                                userID,
                                                userPassword);
    if(!(dbConnection.isClosed( ))){

        // First, let's set up our PreparedStatement. Note that instead of hard-coding
        // data right into the SQL, we put question marks in its place. These are
        // placeholders, waiting for us to add parameters. Note that I'm using
        // TYPE_SCROLL_INSENSITIVE, which lets you move around in the
        // ResultSet (going back to the beginning for instance) and I'm using
        // CONCUR_READ_ONLY to make this a read-only ResultSet (you can't
        // use it to do updates). If I didn't do this, we would only be able to move
        // forward in the ResultSet, never backward, and it wouldn't be read-only.
        // I like my queries to be safely read-only!
        sqlStatement = dbConnection.prepareStatement("select * from accounts
                where lookupName = ? and lookupBirthday = ?",
                ResultSet.TYPE_SCROLL_INSENSITIVE,
                ResultSet.CONCUR_READ_ONLY);
```

```java
        // Now let's add our parameters.  We add them using "set" methods which
        // force the data to conform to the data type we're expecting, like setString
        // (which converts the data into VARCHAR before applying it in the SQL).
        //  The first parameter in each method is the index it corresponds with (the
        // first question mark has an index of 1, the second has 2, and so on).  The
        // second parameter is the value.
        // If a value we pass can't be converted properly, we get a SQLException.
        sqlStatement.setString(1, lookupName);
        sqlStatement.setString(2, lookupBirthday);

        // Now, since we're executing a query, we'll want to retrieve it into a
        // ResultSet object.  ResultSet is very useful, and lets us move around
        // within it, accessing the data and so on. If something goes wrong with
        // the query, we'll get a SQLException.  If no results come back, we'll get
        // back a ResultSet with no records in it.
        queryResults = sqlStatement.executeQuery( );

        // Let's see if we got any rows back. We call next( ), because it returns true if it
        // moves to the first record successfully, and false if there are no records.  ResultSets
        // initially start at the position just before the first record.
        if(queryResults.next( )){

            // Good; there are records.  Move back to the beginnning, because we'll also
            // be using  next( ) as the condition in our while loop. We know at this point
            // that we have at least one record.
            queryResults.beforeFirst( );

            // Now let's process one record at a time, doing something useful; each call to
            // next() pushes the ResultSet to the next database record in the set returned
            // by the query.
            while(queryResults.next( )){

                // DO SOMETHING USEFUL WITH THE RECORD.

                // For example, let's fetch out the value in a column, say, phoneNumber.
                // You can do this by the database table's column name, or by the column
                // index, with counting starting at 1. Here's an example of each approach:
                phoneNumber = queryResults.getString("phoneNumber");
                phoneNumber = queryResults.getString(5);

            }

        } else {

            // No records came back!
            throw(new RuntimeException("No records were returned!"));

        }

    } else {

        // The database connection was closed!  That's no good.
        throw(new RuntimeException("Database Connection failed to open!"));

    }

}
catch(SQLException sqle){

    // Here you would handle a SQL error, probably passing some sort of
    // meaningful message back to the user.  Generally it'll be something like
    // the database connection being lost during the query.  If your query is
    // just not returning any rows, that's not an error; that's a result.
```

```java
}
finally {
    // Remember to make sure your objects aren't null before you access them.
    if(queryResults != null){
        queryResults.close( );
    }
    if(dbConnection != null){
        if(!(dbConnection.isClosed())){
            dbConnection.close( );
        }
    }
    queryResults = null;
    sqlStatement = null;
    dbConnection = null;
    lookupName = null;
    lookupBirthday = null;
    phoneNumber = null;
    databaseURL = null;
    userName = null;
    userPassword = null;
}
```

Note what we did there. First we registered our driver and got our database connection, then we checked to make sure it was open, then we created a PreparedStatement and set the values of its variables, and finally we executed it as a query and worked with the ResultSet we got back. Finally, we closed our database objects and nulled out all our objects.

A ResultSet is what Java uses to hold database query results. The results are actually being read live from the database while you're working with them; you can only interact with the ResultSet while your database connection is open. Here are the useful methods of ResultSet (there are more; check the API reference):

<u>*Useful Methods of Java's ResultSet Object (Query-Related Stuff Only):*</u>

```java
// In the following, please assume we're working with a ResultSet object called someResults,
// and that we've already populated it with data. You'll notice that for plain queries, I use
// only very few of the methods offered by ResultSet; I like to keep things as simple as possible.

// Move to the position before the first record of the ResultSet:
someResults.beforeFirst( );

// Close the ResultSet and release its resources:
someResults.close( );

// Move to the first record in the ResultSet. Note that this method returns true
// if it successfully moves to a record, and false if there are no records to go to:
boolean thereAreRecords = someResults.first( );

// Get a value from the current record; there are get methods for most data types, but
// we'll show some important ones, like String, int, and Date. Note that you can fetch
// based on field number (counting from the left, with the leftmost field as 1) or based
// on the name of the database field as a String:
int apartmentNumber = someResults.getInt(1);
int buildingNumber = someResults.getInt("building_number");
String firstName = someResults.getString(5);
String lastName = someResults.getString("last_name");
Date orderDate = someResults.getDate(3);
Date deliveryDate = someResults.getDate("delivery_date");
```

```
// Move to the last row of the ResultSet.  Note that this method returns  true
// if it successfully moves to a  record, and false if there are no records to go to:
boolean thereAreRecords = someResults.last( );

// Move to the next row (advance forward one row).  Note that this method returns  true
// if it successfully moves to a new record, and false if there are no records to go to.
// Usually, you'll use this one to see if there are any database results:
boolean thereAreRecords = someResults.next( );
```

Here are a couple of tips: First, when you've first retrieved your ResultSet, use an if statement that checks the return value of next() to see if there are any records in it. If there aren't, return an error message to let the user know there were no results. If there are, call beforeFirst() and THEN start a while loop to process your results as I did in the example. If you just plunge into the while loop, you lose the opportunity to tell your user that there weren't any results.

The way you'll usually use a ResultSet is to fetch data, stuff the data in your class variables, and close the ResultSet. In other words, you'll generally only use it to fetch data and store it locally. Don't leave the data sitting in the ResultSet, which takes up a lot of resources. Keep it open only as long as it takes to grab its data. And always explicitly close your ResultSet and null out its variable, so it can be garbage collected.

That's pretty much it for doing simple queries in Java. When all you're doing is reading data, you'll do it that way almost every single time... All of the real complexity comes from your SQL, not your actual Java code, which is very straightforward and almost always looks about the same.

Updating, Inserting, or Deleting From a Database Without ResultSets:

Now let's look at actually updating records in a database. The process itself isn't much more complicated than doing a simple query. You're still going to use a PreparedStatement and you're still going to write SQL code. Everything is more or less the same, with only minor changes here and there.

In the following example, we'll be doing an insert. Note that updates and deletes only differ from inserts in that you'll write different SQL to implement them. In other words, any code that changes the database will look more or less the same except for the SQL you use.

Clear as mud? Consider this example:

SAMPLE CODE: *Inserting to a Database Using a PreparedStatement*
(*updates and deletes work in EXACTLY the same way, only the SQL is different):*

```
// Remember to import java.sql.*; at the top of your class file!
import java.sql.*;

// The rest is assumed to be somewhere within your Java class, like in a method:
// Assume we have already received variables userID and userPassword from the user.

// First, our database connection setup parameters:
String  databaseURL = "jdbc:derby:EXAMPLE";

// Next, Our database related objects:
Connection dbConnection;
PreparedStatement sqlStatement;
int recordsAffected = 0;

// Two sample parameters for our example:
String lookupName = "Joe Smith";
String lookupBirthday = "01-MAY-53";
```

```java
try{
    // Here we open our database Connection.
    Class.forName("org.apache.derby.jdbc.EmbeddedDriver");
    dbConnection = DriverManager.getConnection (databaseURL,
                                                userID,
                                                userPassword);
    if(!(dbConnection.isClosed( ))){
        // First, let's set up our PreparedStatement. Note that instead of hard-coding
        // data right into the SQL, we put question marks in its place.  These are
        // placeholders, waiting for us to add parameters.  Note that I've taken out
        // the two query-related parameters I was using before.
        sqlStatement = dbConnection.prepareStatement("insert into accounts
                    (lookupName, lookupBirthday)values(?, ?)");

        // Now let's add our parameters. We add them using "set" methods which
        // force the data to conform to the data type we're expecting, like setString
        // (which converts the data into VARCHAR before applying it in the SQL).
        // The first parameter in each method is the index it corresponds with (the
        // first question mark has an index of 1, the second has 2, and so on).  The
        // second parameter is the value.
        // If a value we pass can't be converted properly, we get a SQLException.
        sqlStatement.setString(1, lookupName);
        sqlStatement.setString(2, lookupBirthday);

        // Let's go ahead and execute our insert.
        recordsAffected = sqlStatement.executeUpdate( );

        // Let's see if we inserted any rows, since this was an insert. Note that if it was
        // an update or a delete, then maybe it would be ok for no rows to be affected
        // under certain circumstances.  It depends on the situation.
        if(recordsAffected == 1){
            // Hey, alright. Since we succeeded, you'd want to set up a "success"
            // message for your user here. But don't return right away! You still
            // have to clear out your objects down below.
        } else if(recordsAffected > 1) {
            // Too many records were affected!  Throw an exception.
            throw(new RuntimeException("The insert affected too many records!"));
        } else {
            // NO records were affected. Throw an exception.
            throw(new RuntimeException("The insert didn't affect any records!"));
        }
    } else {
        // The database connection was closed!  That's no good.
        throw(new RuntimeException("Database Connection failed to open!"));
    }
}
catch(SQLException sqle){
    // Here you would handle the SQL error, probably passing some sort of
    // meaningful message back to the user.  Generally it'll be something like
    // the user not having sufficient privileges to view a table.
```

```
    }
    finally {

        if(dbConnection != null){
            if(!(dbConnection.isClosed())){
                dbConnection.close( );
            }
        }
        sqlStatement = null;
        dbConnection = null;
        lookupName = null;
        lookupBirthday = null;
        phoneNumber = null;
        databaseURL = null;
        userName = null;
        userPassword = null;
        recordsAffected = 0;
    }
```

That's all there is to it. It's pretty easy, not that big a deal at all. It doesn't even require much code. Most of the lines of code in the above examples dealt with error handling and clearing out objects once you're done with the task at hand.

Now that we've discussed queries and updates, let's talk about something a little more amusing: transactions.

Database Transactions:

Database transactions are sets of SQL instructions that either succeed or fail as a unit. Either the whole set of commands succeeds (and are "committed"), or they're all reversed ("rolled back"). They're important whenever you're making multiple changes to a database and some of the changes depend on other changes. For example, let's say you're taking an order from a client. One database table has information about the product that's being purchased and another has information about how the order's going to be carried out. A third table has information about payment details. If the first two tables are updated successfully but the third table isn't, you might want to undo the entire set of changes and report the error to the clerk using the software.

In Java, transactions are easy to work with. By default, database connections under Java are in "autoCommit" mode. This means that each statement you execute is automatically committed right away, and considered to be its own individual transaction. In order to run multiple SQL statements in a single transaction, just turn autoCommit off while you're running the statements. To do this, assuming you have a database connection called dbConnection, call the method "dbConnection.setAutoCommit(false);" and you'll have turned off autoCommit. Make sure you use the same connection for all the statements you want to run. Once all of the statements have been executed, if any of them have failed, call "dbConnection.rollback();" and your transaction will be rolled back. On the other hand, if they've all succeeded, call "dbConnection.commit();" and you'll commit your transaction. Once you're completely done, call "dbConnection.setAutoCommit(true);" to return your connection to autoCommit mode.

Here's a quick example of JUST the transactional part of a three-part insert; assume the connection is dbConnection, the PreparedStatement is sqlStatement, there's an int recordsAffected, and we're inserting a customer's name and ID into three tables (accounts, orders, and receipts). Note that I'm throwing a custom exception to bring the code down to a catch block, where I can handle all errors with the same chunk of code. This way, whether there's an actual failure (like a bad connection) or something simpler happens (an insert doesn't work), it all gets handled the same way.

SAMPLE CODE: *Modifying a database insert to be transactional:*

```java
try{
    // Assume dbConnection and sqlStatement have already been set up.
    dbConnection.setAutoCommit(false);
    sqlStatement = dbConnection.prepareStatement("insert into accounts(name,id)
                                                    values(?,?)");
    sqlStatement.setString(1,"Joe");
    sqlStatement.setString(2,"ABC123");
    recordsAffected = sqlStatement.executeUpdate( );

    if(recordsAffected == 1) {

        // Then we know the first command worked; we proceed.

        sqlStatement = dbConnection.prepareStatement("insert into orders(name,id)
                                                        values(?,?)");
        sqlStatement.setString(1,"Joe");
        sqlStatement.setString(2,"ABC123");
        recordsAffected = sqlStatement.executeUpdate( );

        if(recordsAffected == 1){

            // Then this one worked also. We continue.
            sqlStatement = dbConnection.prepareStatement("insert into receipts(name,id)
                                                            values(?,?)");
            sqlStatement.setString(1,"Joe");
            sqlStatement.setString(2,"ABC123");
            recordsAffected = sqlStatement.executeUpdate( );
            if(recordsAffected == 1){
                // This one has also worked. We're done; we commit.
                dbConnection.commit( );
            } else {
                dbConnection.rollback;   // Rollback on failure.
            }

        } else {
            dbConnection.rollback; // Rollback on failure.
        }

    } else {
        dbConnection.rollback; // Rollback on failure.
    }

}
catch(SQLException re){

    // We threw a SQL exception. Here you would react to the SQLException somehow,
    // but because this is transactional, you can't just throw it up to the calling code;
    // you have to do a rollback FIRST. You can wrap it and throw a custom exception
    // if you want.

    dbConnection.rollback( );
    dbConnection.setAutoCommit(true);

}
finally {

    // Last step: turn AutoCommit back on, especially if you're reusing the connection (we're not).
    dbConnection.setAutoCommit(true);

    if(dbConnection != null){
        if(!(dbConnection.isClosed( ))){
```

```
            dbConnection.close( );
        }
    }
    dbConnection = null;
    sqlStatement = null;
}
```

One thing you should keep in mind about transactions is, if an exception happens when you're part-way through the transaction, will your code actually do the rollback? Or will it just throw the Exception up to the calling code? The situation is little trickier, because you don't want to leave the database in an inconsistent state. If you throw the exception upwards without doing a rollback, the database will be left waiting for the transaction to complete, and it'll probably time out. Make sure your code always either commits its changes or rolls them back. This means, don't throw checked exceptions and be extra careful about nulls, so you don't get any unexpected RuntimeExceptions.

That concludes *almost* everything you'll need to do day-to-day work with JDBC and a database. These techniques are good enough for most of the tasks you'll have to do on a regular basis. But there's one more bit of information I'd like to share with you. It concerns the subject of "row locking".

When you're doing a database insert, the previous techniques are *always* good enough, because *inserts don't affect existing records*. Nobody else can tamper with a record that doesn't exist yet, right? But when you're viewing, updating, or deleting *existing* records, it's possible for someone else to come along behind the scenes and alter the record while you're working with it. For example, let's say you have a set of data that is shared among several users. One user queries the database and pulls up a record. While he's looking at it, another user pulls up the same record. The first user changes the record and saves his work; ten minutes later, the other user does the same thing. The second user has no way of knowing that the first user was accessing the record, or that his changes will overwrite those made by the first user. The two users may end up rather annoyed at each other later on, or at least, they'll be annoyed at the poor programmer (YOU) who built the system.

On the other hand, if you *lock* the record when the first user opens it, the second user won't be able to update the record; for him, it'll be read-only. He'll know someone else is working on it, and the whole misunderstanding will be avoided. Ideally, he'll ask around to see who's working on that record, and the two of them will be able to talk about how to proceed without stepping on each other's toes.

In order to perform a select, update, or delete while locking the rows, you'll need to take a few steps. First, you'll need to formulate a select query that fetches the row or rows you want to view, update, or delete (don't bother with all this work for inserts; those don't require the additional attention). Next, you'll need to tack the words "for update" to the end of the SQL query (this is what actually locks the rows). Then, you'll want to set up your ResultSet so it's updatable, and make sure your database connection doesn't autoCommit any changes (if autoCommit is turned on, the minute you make a change the lock is released and the ResultSet is closed, which ruins the whole process). Finally, you'll want to fetch the data, leaving it in the ResultSet while you work on it, use the update methods of ResultSet to perform your work, and either commit or roll back your changes.

Here's a bit of tested source code that illustrates how to update two tables using this technique. I ran this within NetBeans, and checked to make sure the database was being updated properly. Rollbacks worked also. This is a very simple example, of course, but it gets the idea across:

EXAMPLE: Using a ResultSet to Lock Rows While Working With Them:

```
package philsexperiments;

import java.sql.*;

/**
 * Generic experimental project. I use this to test code.
 * @author pperry
 */
public class Main {
```

```java
public Main() {
}

public static void main(String[] args) {

    // Just calls the method that tests the technique... No big deal.
    testRowLockingUpdates();

}


/** The purpose of this method is to try out a way
 * of doing database updates that keeps rows locked
 * while they're being worked on. I'm not certain
 * that this is beneficial or necessary, though. I
 * need to consider this in more depth.  Still, I'd
 * like to know HOW to do it, even if I never choose to.
 *
 * This code assumes I've got two dumb little database tables:
 *
 * PEOPLE:
 * PERSON_ID     PERSON_DESCRIPTION      PERSON_IMPORTANCE
 * 1             Joe Simmons             85
 * 2             Howard Beech            35
 * 3             Joel Beech              45
 *
 * PLACES:
 * PLACE_ID   PERSON_ID (fk)   PLACE_DESCRIPTION     PLACE_IMPORTANCE
 * 1          1                Simmons's Pad         75
 * 2          1                Simmons's Other Pad   77
 * 3          2                Beech's Place         62
 * 4          3                Joel's Apt.           40
 *
 * The following sample code is EXTREMELY dumb and simple, and
 * does no real error-checking, but it ran in NetBeans, so it's
 * a valid example of how to use updatable ResultSets...
 *
 * Note that the point of doing updates this way, as opposed to
 * just using a straight SQL Update statement, is that while we're
 * working on these records, we're actually LOCKING them. In "real
 * life", you'd probably only use this when a user has to open a
 * record, view the data, make some changes, and save the data,
 * all while being CERTAIN that nobody else can mess with it while
 * he's working on it. This technique locks the rows while you've
 * got the ResultSet open, and only releases the lock when you
 * commit or rollback (or when the ResultSet is closed).
 *
 * @author: Philip Perry
 */
public static void testRowLockingUpdates(){

    String databaseURL = "jdbc:derby:C:\\PhilsTestArea\\PhilsMiniExperimentDB";
    String userID = "Phil";
    String userPassword = "PhilsMiniExperimentDB";
    Connection dbConnection = null;
```

```java
        PreparedStatement prepStatement;
        ResultSet queryResults;
        String SQLQueryText;

        try{

            // Register the derby driver...
            Class.forName("org.apache.derby.jdbc.EmbeddedDriver");

            // Get a database connection...
            dbConnection = DriverManager.getConnection(databaseURL,
                                                    userID,
                                                    userPassword);

            // Make the connection transactional...
            dbConnection.setAutoCommit(false);

            // Create a PreparedStatement that will return an updatable ResultSet
            // that locks rows...
            SQLQueryText = " SELECT * FROM PHIL_TEST.PEOPLE WHERE " +
                        "PERSON_ID=? FOR UPDATE";
            prepStatement = dbConnection.prepareStatement(SQLQueryText,
                            ResultSet.TYPE_SCROLL_INSENSITIVE,
                            ResultSet.CONCUR_UPDATABLE);

            // Set the parameter for the prepared statement...
            prepStatement.setInt(1, 1);

            // Execute as a query to get the ResultSet we want...
            queryResults = prepStatement.executeQuery();

            // Move to the first (only, in this case) row:
            queryResults.next();

            // Update the description field to show we've altered the database...
            queryResults.updateString("PERSON_DESCRIPTION", "Joe Simmons updated!");
            queryResults.updateInt("PERSON_IMPORTANCE", 90);

            // Call updateRow to update the database...
            queryResults.updateRow();

            // Close the ResultSet so we can reuse the variable...
            queryResults.close();

            // Create a second prepared statement to update a record in a second table...
            SQLQueryText = "SELECT * FROM PHIL_TEST.PLACES WHERE " +
                        "PLACE_ID=? FOR UPDATE";
            prepStatement = dbConnection.prepareStatement(SQLQueryText,
                            ResultSet.TYPE_SCROLL_INSENSITIVE,
                            ResultSet.CONCUR_UPDATABLE);

            // Set the parameter...
            prepStatement.setInt(1, 2);

            // Execute as a query to get a ResultSet...
            queryResults = prepStatement.executeQuery();
```

```java
        // Move to the first (hopefully only) record:
        queryResults.next();

        // Update the description field to show we've altered the database...
        queryResults.updateString("PLACE_DESCRIPTION", "Simmons Other Pad updated!");
        queryResults.updateInt("PLACE_IMPORTANCE", 75);

        // Call updateRow to update the database...
        queryResults.updateRow();

        // Close the ResultSet out...
        queryResults.close();

        // And commit.
        dbConnection.commit();

    } // try
    catch(SQLException e){

        // Something went wrong. Roll it back.
        if(dbConnection != null){
            if(!(dbConnection.isClosed())){
                dbConnection.rollback();
            }
        }
        // Always do the rollback first, then other stuff... It's safer.
        System.out.println("ERROR! " + e.getMessage());

    } // catch

} // testRowLockingUpdates

} // Main
```

Usually, the regular techniques will be enough; people will be altering their own data, and there won't be that much overlap between different users. But you'll end up in situations where you'll want to be able to lock the rows you're working on, and with this approach, you'll be able to do so.

Note that a REAL test of row locking would involve trying to hit the records using more than one client, and seeing if the second client is made to wait (and noting what happens when the lock is released, etc). My goal here has been just to show you how to do row locking, so I kept it simple.

Chapter 8: Collections (the ArrayList and the HashMap)

In this almost-last chapter I'd like to add some notes on two Java objects I use frequently: the ArrayList and the HashMap. Both are collections, and both are much more interesting and useful than arrays. In fact, you will usually not want to use an array when you can use one of these instead.

An ArrayList is a much more useful and powerful form of array that makes it very easy to implement any type of list you want. Need a stack? A queue? It's a piece of cake, with hardly any code involved. A HashMap is like a Perl Hash, in that it contains name/value pairs. Put these two things together and you've got a nice bit of local storage for managing any sort of data that's organized by rows and columns. Let's start by looking at the ArrayList.

The ArrayList

An ArrayList is like an array in some ways. It's a linear set of objects, indexed, which you can scan through. It is also much more powerful. You can add objects to the front of the list, to the rear, or to an indexed position in the middle, or you can delete objects from any position. When you make these changes, the ArrayList automatically adjusts itself, closing gaps and expanding to hold new entries. Think of an ArrayList as an array on steroids; it's an array that anticipates everything you might want to do with it.

In order to use an ArrayList, you have to import the ArrayList class and make it available to your code. Use this statement:

Making ArrayList available to your code:
import java.util.ArrayList;

Once you've imported ArrayList, you have to declare an ArrayList variable. In olden times (before Java 1.5) there was just a plain-old ArrayList, which contained plain-old Objects. When you retrieved an object from the ArrayList, you had to manually cast the object to the type you were expecting. This looked like this:

Old-Style ArrayList With Manual Cast:
ArrayList aListOfObjects = new ArrayList();

aListOfObjects.add(new String("This is a test"));

String tempString = (String) aListOfObjects.get(0);

That approach to working with ArrayLists was pretty comfortable, but Sun improved on it a while back; ever since Java 1.5, we've had "generics", i.e. the ability to declare an ArrayList to hold a specific type of object. All we have to do is insert the object type, between angle brackets, in the declaration. The syntax for declaring an ArrayList that holds a specific type of object looks like this:

Declaring but not instantiating an ArrayList Object while specifying the object type:
ArrayList < `object type` > `array list name`;

Example:

ArrayList <String> aListOfStrings;

Declaring and instantiating an ArrayList object while specifying the object type,:
ArrayList < `object type` > `array list name` = **new** ArrayList< `object type` >( );
Example:
ArrayList <String> aListOfStrings = new ArrayList<String>( );

    Since the ArrayList is now able to be targeted at a specific type of object, you can retrieve the objects contained in the ArrayList without manually casting them to the type they should be. I never minded casting, myself, but I like the new approach.

    Regardless of which approach you've used (the old one is still available), once you've declared and instantiated your ArrayList, you'll want to actually DO something with it. ArrayLists offer a number of useful methods; I'll show you the ones I find useful by example. Let's assume you're still working with the String-oriented ArrayList from the last example. Note that, like arrays, ArrayLists index their elements starting with zero (0).

Methods Available in ArrayList:
```
// In the following examples, assume we've declared and instantiated an ArrayList called
// aListOfStrings. Assume that we've set it up to target String objects and that we've pre-
// populated it with a number of Strings for our use. Finally, assume that we have declared
// a string variable "tempString" to help us work with our ArrayList.
```

// *Adding a new String to the end of the ArrayList (i.e. the highest index):*
tempString = "This is a test.";
aListOfStrings.add(tempString);

// *Adding a new String to the ArrayList at position 4 (counting starts at 0):*
tempString = "This is a test.";
aListOfStrings.add(4, tempString);

// *Adding a whole ArrayList of Strings, for example a second ArrayList called*
// *"anotherListOfStrings" to the end of our ArrayList:*
aListOfStrings.addAll(anotherListOfStrings);

// *Adding a whole ArrayList of Strings at position 4 in our ArrayList:*
aListOfStrings.addAll(4, anotherListOfStrings);

// *Fetching a String from the fourth position in the ArrayList:*
String tempString = aListOfStrings.get(4);

// *Removing the String at the fourth position in the ArrayList:*
aListOfStrings.remove(4);

// *Removing a whole range of indices, inclusive, from the ArrayList:*
aListOfStrings.remove(firstIndex, lastIndex);

// *Clearing out the entire list:*
aListOfStrings.clear( );

// *Setting the value of the specific element at index 4 with a new String (replacement):*
tempString = "This is another test.";
aListOfStrings.set(4, tempString);

// *See how many elements are currently in the ArrayList:*
int numberOfElements;
numberOfElements = aListOfStrings.size( );

```
// See whether the ArrayList actually has anything in it:
boolean isItEmpty;
isItEmpty = aListOfStrings.isEmpty( );

// Return an Array of the same type as the object in the ArrayList:
String [ ] tempArray;
tempArray = aListOfStrings.toArray( );
```

ArrayLists are useful whenever you have a list of objects you want to keep together and process sequentially. For example, you might want to retrieve a list of all the Employee objects for a given department, sorted by employee ID. They're also useful for implementing "stacks" and "queues". Let's talk about those briefly, and how you would use an ArrayList to implement them. I'm not going to get into a whole discussion of data structures, but these particular structures are very useful.

A stack is a "last in, first out" list; you add new elements to the end of the list, and when it's time to remove an element from the list, you do so starting at the end as well, so the last element you inserted is the first you remove. You would use a stack in recursion, for example, if you wanted to store some kind of name or description each time you recurse into the method you're running (maybe so you can display it to the user?). Every time you enter the method, you'd "push" a new String onto the end of the list, and as each method finishes what it's doing and returns back up a level, you'd "pop" an element from the end of the list, showing your description (or whatever) to the user. Check out this example:

Implementing a Stack Using ArrayList, and just because I'm bored, recursion:

```
// First, let's assume we've got the following method description; it's static so I
// can try it out in my toy test rig's public static void main method:
static void stackUpAndDown(ArrayList <String> myToyStack, int i){

    if(i < 10){     // <-- Our control variable, i, ends the recursion at i = 10.

        // These first three statements create the message and push it on the
        // stack, then recursively call stackUpAndDown. This process builds
        // the stack -- note that we don't get past the method call until i >= 10
        // and the deepest method call (level 9, here) returns.
        String description = "Level " + Integer.toString(i);
        myToyStack.add(description);
        stackUpAndDown(myToyStack, i+1);
        // After stackUpAndDown has returned void, we continue. Note that
        // we're doing a stack "pop" here -- we're getting the last item, then
        // removing it from the stack.
        System.out.println(myToyStack.get(myToyStack.size( ) -1));
        myToyStack.remove(myToyStack.size( ) - 1);

    }
}
// Now, in the main method of a test project in NetBeans, we call this method and let it
// recurse:
stackUpAndDown(new ArrayList<String>( ), 0);

// Here's the output I got when I tested this in NetBeans:
Level 9
Level 8
Level 7
Level 6
Level 5
Level 4
```

Level 3
Level 2
Level 1
Level 0

// The descriptions were stuffed into the stack in order from 0 through 9. We
// retrieved them in last in, first out order. I.E. as a stack. Now admit it; is that
// the shortest useful example of a stack you've ever seen, or what?

    Ok, so now you've seen the jist of a stack; you add things to the end, and you retrieve them from the end. Pretty easy. Now let's look at a queue. Queues are just like stacks, except that they're first in, first out lists, and instead of "push" and "pop", we say "enqueue" and "dequeue". They work like a line at the grocery store; the first person in line is the first person served. Here's our previous example, changed to a queue:

Implementing a Queue Using ArrayList, and just because I'm bored, recursion:

```
// First, let's assume we've got the following method description; it's static so I
// can try it out in my toy test rig's public static void main method:
static void queueUpAndDown(ArrayList <String> myToyQueue, int i){

    if(i < 10){     // <-- Our control variable, i, ends the recursion at i = 10.

        // These first three statements create the message and enqueue it
        // then recursively call queueUpAndDown. This process builds
        // the queue-- note that we don't get past the method call until i >= 10
        // and the deepest method call (level 9, here) returns.
        String description = "Level " + Integer.toString(i);
        myToyQueue.add(description);
        queueUpAndDown(myToyQueue, i+1);
        // After queueUpAndDown has returned void, we continue. Note that
        // we're doing a "dequeue" here -- we're getting the first item, then
        // removing it from the stack.
        System.out.println(myToyQueue.get(0));
        myToyQueue.remove(0);

    }
}
```

// Now, in the main method of a test project in NetBeans, we call this method and let it
// recurse:
queueUpAndDown(new ArrayList<String>( ), 0);

// Here's the output I got when I tested this in NetBeans:
Level 0
Level 1
Level 2
Level 3
Level 4
Level 5
Level 6
Level 7
Level 8
Level 9

// The descriptions were stuffed into the queue in order from 0 through 9. We
// retrieved them in first in, first out order. I.E. as a queue. Now admit it; is that
// the shortest useful example of a queue you've ever seen, or what?

So that about wraps it up for ArrayList, and two neat ways of using it, as a stack and a queue. When I was in college my C++ course had us implement a stack and a queue the old way, as C++ classes, with push, pop, enqueue and dequeue methods, pointers, and references. ArrayList literally hands you both of these data structures on a silver platter; it's nice.

The HashMap:

HashMaps are really easy to understand. They're just collections of key/value pairs. Anytime you have a set of data which can be sorted into key/value pairs, you can stick it in a HashMap.

Now, originally, HashMaps dealt with Objects only, so when you pulled your data back out you'd have to do an explicit cast, just as with ArrayList. Since Java 1.5, we've been able to declare a HashMap to target a specific type of class for the key and a different type of class for the value. For example, you could store Strings in the key, and some other type of object in the value. In my opinion, 9 times out of 10, you're going to want to use a String as both key and value, and you'll use the HashMap as a simple lookup table. Another thing you might do is use a String for key and an object of your own design as the value. If you ever DO use one of your own objects as a key, you'll have to implement comparable, which might be more trouble than it's worth for this sort of thing.

In order to use a HashMap in your code, first you have to import the HashMap package, which is in java.util just like ArrayList:

Importing java.util.HashMap:
import java.util.HashMap;

Next, you'll have to declare and instantiate a HashMap object, which can be done the old way, targeting plain Objects, or the new way, defining an object type for both key and value. Note that there are several constructors for HashMap, but you'll generally ignore them and use the default constructor because it's all you need. First, let's look at the plain-object approach:

Declaring but not Instantiating a HashMap using plain Objects:
HashMap `hash_map_name`;

// Example:

HashMap myHashMap;

Declaring and Instantiating a HashMap Using Plain Objects:
HashMap `hash_map_name` = new HashMap( );

// Example:

HashMap myHashMap = new HashMap( );

Pretty simple, right? In order to work with a HashMap you've instantiated this way, you have to do an explicit cast whenever you retrieve an object from the HashMap. For example, let's say you've stored Strings in your key/value pairs, and that one specific pair of Strings is "Dave" and "Mullet" (for the guy and his haircut, respectively). You want to fetch Dave's haircut type back out of the HashMap. You would do something like this:

Example: Retrieving a key/value pair from HashMap using an explicit cast:
`data_type` `variable_name` = (`data_type`) `hash_map_name`.get(" `key` ");

// Example:
String haircut = (String) myHashMap.get("Dave");

Note that because Objects are more generic than Strings, you don't generally have to do a cast when you're putting things INTO the HashMap. Pretty simple, right? Of course, if you're using Java 1.5 or later, you can specify the object types held in the HashMap and you don't have to do the cast, which is nice. Here's a pair of examples related to the 1.5 and later generics approach:

Declaring but not instantiating a HashMap with defined object type for key and value:
HashMap<<u>key object type</u>, <u>value object type</u>> <u>hash map name</u>;
// Example:
HashMap <String, String> myHashMap;

Declaring and instantiating a HashMap with defined object type for key and value:
HashMap <<u>key object type</u>, <u>value object type</u>> <u>hash map name</u> =
      new **HashMap** <<u>key object type</u>, <u>value object type</u>> ( );
// Example:
HashMap <String, String> myHashMap = new HashMap<String, String>( );

Basically it works very similarly to an ArrayList, only instead of a list of objects, you've got key-value pairs of objects. Let's look at examples showing some of the useful methods available in HashMap; for these examples, assume you've declared and filled a HashMap called "myHashMap" and that it's been defined to use Strings for keys and values:

Examples: useful method calls available in HashMap:
// How to clear out your HashMap (remove all key-value pairs):
myHashMap.clear( );

// How to see whether the HashMap contains a specific key String "Dave":
boolean isItInthere = myHashMap.containsKey("Dave");

// How to see whether the HashMap contains a specific value String "Mullet":
boolean isItInThere = myHashMap.containsValue("Mullet");

// How to get the value associated with a specific key String:
String returnedValue = myHashMap.get("Dave");

// How to see if the HashMap is empty or not:
boolean isItEmpty = myHashMap.isEmpty( );

// How to see how big the HashMap is (i.e. get the number of key-value pairs):
int howBigIsIt = myHashMap.size( );

// How to put a new key-value pair into the HashMap:
myHashMap.put("Dave", "Mullet");

// How to remove a key-value pair from the HashMap:
myHashMap.remove("Dave");

// How to stick all the key-value pairs from another HashMap into your HashMap
// (Try to make the two HashMaps compatible, as far as their key-value objects go):
myHashMap.putAll(someOtherHashMap);

// How to grab an ArrayList of all the keys in your HashMap -- note that this method
// returns a "Set," the keyset, that is still tied to the HashMap. This means that any changes
// you make to the keyset (like removing an element) will ALSO affect the HashMap, which
// is generally a rotten idea. If you remove one of the elements of the keyset, the key-value
// pair that goes with it disappears from the HashMap.
// <u>BUT</u>, if you use the keyset to create a new ArrayList, the ArrayList will contain a list of
// references to the keys in the keymap, and will NOT be directly tied to the HashMap.
// I just tested this in NetBeans, and removing an element from the ArrayList does NOT
// remove it from the HashMap; it just removes the reference in the ArrayList. So this is
// a whole lot safer. Here's how to do it:
ArrayList mySetOfKeys = new ArrayList(myHashMap.keyset( ));

// Note that you can also grab a list of values, but in practice, I can't think of any reason
// WHY you would want to; almost everything is organized by key, right? What
// good is an unsorted list of values without the keys that give them context? If you need
// this, you can find it in the API ref, but I'd be surprised if you did.

HashMaps are pretty useful tools, particularly if you want to retrieve initialization information for your software and use it ad hoc while your program runs. You can also use it to store the contents of a database record, with the keys representing the names of table columns and the values the column's data. Or maybe you want to do something like associate server names with IP addresses, having loaded these in from a file or database query at runtime. Anything that is suited to being stored as key-value pairs can be held in a HashMap.

In closing, I'd like to point out that there are numerous other data structures, like Maps, Sets, and trees. You may over time find use for these other structures; if so, look the API reference over and you'll find many to choose from. In the meantime, I think these two data structures will give you what you need in most cases, particularly if you're doing applications programming.

Chapter 9: Threads

Technically, Java threads are an advanced topic, but they're so useful I couldn't leave them out of this book. Also, if you take the easy approach and implement "Runnable", they're not hard to work with. I'll give you some very straightforward code to look at that will make implementing threads in your software relatively easy. This code is from a real working project, so it's a nice example to work with.

Let's start with the obvious question: what is a "thread"? Simply put, a thread is a set of memory, processor time, and resources an operating system lets your software allocate (use) when you run it. In other words, software runs in threads, and usually, allocates more than one at a time, stuffing important subprograms in their own threads so the software's users don't have to be interrupted when the subprogram is busy.

This ability to run multiple threads is important; it's not just a convenience for the user, it's what makes software usable. If programs were only able to occupy a single thread, every time a program had to do something time consuming its user would have to sit and wait. If the user wanted to open a file, he'd have to wait a few minutes before he could interact with his computer again. If he wanted to download a file from a website, he might have to wait for hours or even days. Even the simplest activities would take much too long; people would get fed up and go back to using paper and post-it notes.

Luckily, modern operating systems (and especially languages like Java) allow programmers to set up their software so it allocates and uses multiple threads simultaneously. Their users can continue working with the software running in the main thread while other threads are "spawned" to do time consuming or resource intensive grunt work. Of course, a really busy thread will still slow a computer down.

In order to work with threads, all you have to do is implement the "Runnable" interface in a class that will be doing resource-intensive work. In that class, you'll have to provide a "run" method that will start executing when the thread is created. Finally, you'll have to create your new thread and "start" it in your main body of code (the original thread from which the new thread is spawned).

Telling you about it won't be enough to make it clear to you what's going on, so let's jump right into the sample code; I've stripped out everything except the thread-related stuff, and commented about what's going on, so this should be all the example you need:

Example: The Class whose work will be run in a newly spawned thread:

```java
// The code from which I stripped this example was designed to
// read large import files and insert them to a database after
// parsing and rearranging them. It was very resource intensive
// and before I moved it to its own thread, the software would
// basically lock up and I'd have to wait for the imports to finish.

import java.lang.StringBuffer;

// Step 1 is to have your class implement the interface "Runnable".
public class HandleImportsInThread implements Runnable {

    // This StringBuffer will be used to pass a status message back to the
    // original thread. StringBuffers are thread-safe, and since they're
    // mutable, you can add status messages to them without losing
    // the reference to the original StringBuffer. You can't do this with
    // a regular String, because when you change a String, you create
    // a whole new String, losing the reference to the original one.
    protected StringBuffer returnMessages;

    // This is a regular constructor; it works normally.
    public HandleImportsInThread(StringBuffer returnMessages_IN) {
```

```
            returnMessages = returnMessages_IN;
    }

    // Here's the method that does the work of the new thread.
    // It starts automatically when the newly spawned thread
    // starts executing.
    public void run() {

        // Here you would put the code that, being time
        // consuming or resource intensive, should be run
        // in a thread. Common examples would be reading
        // large files, accessing resources over a slow
        // web connection, stuff like that.

        // To pass status information back, append it to returnMessages.
    }

}
```

So, that's relatively simple. First, implement Runnable, then create an implementation of the method "run" and put all your thread-specific code in there. When the class is instantiated and run in a newly spawned thread, the run method will be called and your code will execute.

Generally, what you'll want to do is set up your resource-intensive task as a simple sequential set of instructions and put them in the run method. In order to have your main thread know something about the status of whatever operation your new thread is working on, you can pass a reference to a thread-safe object to the above object via its constructor and update it with a message about the results. For example, above we're using a StringBuffer to return a status, because StringBuffers are mutable; even if you change them, the reference variable in the new thread AND the reference variable in the old thread will still be pointing at the same object in memory (NOTE: This won't work with a regular String! Strings are immutable, so when you update them, you create a whole new String -- this breaks the connection to the object owned by the original thread).

Now let's look at how the new thread is spawned in the main body of code. On the next page, you'll see the code in the main thread that actually spawns the child thread the previously shown Runnable class will run in. Note that in it, we don't call the "run" method of our Runnable class. We call the "start" method of the Thread class. The "run" method gets called automatically by the new thread. Check out this example:

Example: the code that spawns the new thread:

```
// Our imports.
import java.lang.StringBuffer;
import java.lang.Thread;

public class MainThread {

    // Here's our status message carrying StringBuffer. We'll pass a reference
    // to this object to the object we're going to run in the new thread. We'll
    // update the StringBuffer in the new thread, and when the thread finishes
    // executing, we'll be able to check our status back here.
    StringBuffer statusMessage;

    // In the constructor, nothing special; initialize our StringBuffer.
    public MainThread( )
```

```
            statusMessage = new StringBuffer( );
    }
    // Here's the method that kicks off the new thread:
    public runTheImport( ){

        try{

            // First, we instantiate our Runnable class:
            HandleImportsInThread localImportHandler =
                                    new HandleImportsInThread(statusMessage);

            // Next, we instantiate a thread, passing it our Runnable class:
            Thread importHandlerThread = new Thread(localImportHandler);

            // Finally, we call the start( ) method in our new thread.
            importHandlerThread.start( );

            // And that's it!  The new thread is now running separately from this, the
            // old thread. We can continue on here, with the other thread running in
            // the background.

        }
        catch(IllegalThreadStateException e){

            // Of course, no plan is perfect. If something goes wrong, there'll be
            // an exception. Catch it, and handle it.
            statusMessage.append("Oi! It broke, eh? No threads for you!");

        }
    }
}
```

And that's enough information to get started writing your own threads. There are other ways to do it, for instance by extending Thread itself, but I've always found implementing Runnable to be easy and clean and have never been tempted to do threads any other way.

Here's a neat trick, before we move on to our last chapter. If you're working on a program with a graphical user interface, you can actually pass references to the components of your GUI when you instantiate your new thread (instead of using a StringBuffer). Then your new thread can actually update your main thread's GUI, for example, updating a progress bar. Not only do you get to let your user keep working, but you get to show him some eye candy too. One peculiarity I've noticed about human nature is this: if your software is loading a file but there's no status bar, your users will think it takes many times as long as it really does. But if there IS a status bar, their sense of the passing of time will be much more accurate, or at least reasonable. Keep your users happy; give 'em a status bar and load files in a separate thread.

Chapter 10: A Very Short Chapter on Java Date Manipulation:

In Java, there are three objects you'll want to be familiar with if you want to work with dates and times: the Date, Calendar, and DateFormat objects. They're relatively easy to use, and they're good enough to handle most of the things a normal programmer will have to do in his daily work.

While you're reading this section, please keep in mind that I'm trying to keep things as simple as possible. There are probably a million other ways in which you can manipulate dates and times, and many of these are much more sophisticated than the stuff I'm going to show you. If you want to delve in further, just browse your API reference and experiment with the various methods that are available to you. This extremely short chapter should be enough to get you started, though.

First, a little history. Originally, there was just the Date object. It stored dates the Unix way, i.e. as a long that held the number of milliseconds since the "Epoch" (12:00 AM, January 1st, 1970). This Epoch is considered the standard under Unix, Java, and POSIX. Consider it the "beginning of the modern era" as far as Java is concerned.

The Date object was great, and offered many useful methods to manipulate dates, but from what I've been reading online, it wasn't considered easy to expand for international use. It seems that there were issues with the codebase that would have made it difficult to expand it to handle multiple locales; it was easier to build some new objects around Date and make those more flexible, so that's what everyone did. That's probably a huge oversimplification, but that's my understanding of what happened based on the few things I've been reading about it.

Anyway, instead of working out all the issues with the Date object itself, two new objects were created: Calendar, which provides most of the date adjustment and manipulation methods, and DateFormat, which provides formatting methods.

The idea since Java 1.1 seems to be that you use a Date object just to hold the value of the date itself, you use Calendar to perform operations on dates, and you use DateFormat to set up how you want the dates to look when you show them to a user. In other words, Date is used for internal storage, Calendar provides tools, and DateFormat adjusts a date's appearance.

The methods of Date that used to perform all these tasks have been deprecated. Use them at your own risk. Now, let's get into some actual how-to info. I'll keep this short but sweet.

Working With Dates and Times in Java:

```
// To work with dates, start out by importing the following packages:

import java.util.Date;
import java.text.DateFormat;
import java.util.Calendar;

// First, let's look at how to get the current time and date so you can set a timestamp:

// Use a Calendar object to get the current time, in the current time zone and locale,
// and pass it to a Date object:
Calendar tempCal = Calendar.getInstance();
Date tempDate = tempCal.getTime();

// Use a Calendar object, but this time set a SPECIFIC date, then pass it to a Date object:
Calendar tempCal = Calendar.getInstance();
// In Java, months are zero based; below we use "0" for "January":
int year = 2008;
```

```
int month = 0;
int day = 1;
tempCal.set(year, month, day);
Date tempDate = tempCal.getTime();

// Use a Calendar object, but this time set a SPECIFIC date AND time, then pass it to
// a Date object:
Calendar tempCal = Calendar.getInstance();
// In Java, months are zero based; below we use "0" for "January":
int year = 2008;
int month = 0;
int day = 1;
int hour = 23;
int minute = 59;
tempCal.set(year, month, day, hour, minute);
Date tempDate = tempCal.getTime();

// Use a Calendar object, but this time set a SPECIFIC date AND time all the way down
// to the seconds field, then pass it to a Date object:
Calendar tempCal = Calendar.getInstance();
// In Java, months are zero based; below we use "0" for "January":
int year = 2008;
int month = 0;
int day = 1;
int hour = 23;
int minute = 59;
int second = 59;
tempCal.set(year, month, day, hour, minute, second);
Date tempDate = tempCal.getTime();

// By the way, if you want to use constants for the month field, Calendar offers them.
// For example, you can use Calendar.JANUARY instead of 0.  Use all caps.

// If you've already got a Date object set up, you can use it to generate your Calendar
// object (Assume we've received a Date object called tempDate from somewhere):
Calendar tempCal = Calendar.getInstance();
tempCal.setTime(tempDate);

// There are many other methods in Calendar that you might find useful (check the API
// reference). For now, you know how to create a basic Calendar and populate a Date
// object using it.  Now, how about doing some useful things with your Calendar and
// Date objects?

// First, you can get a big timestamp String from a Date object:
String dateAsText = tempDate.toString();

// Second, if you've got a Calendar object (let's call it tempCal) you can retrieve any
// of the Calendar's fields (this is useful when you're building a String that incorporates
// some Date information):

// NOTE: The month field is zero based, so January is the 0th month.
int currentMonth = tempCal.get(Calendar.MONTH);

// Fetching the day is straightforward.
int currentDay = tempCal.get(Calendar.DAY_OF_MONTH);
```

```java
// NOTE: This is different from the deprecated Date method that fetched the year.  The
// OLD version fetched the number of years between the current year and 1900, so if it's
// 1999, you'd get back 99.  The Calendar version gives you the actual year, i.e. 1999,
// which is much better of course -- for one thing, it's Y2K compliant.
int currentYear = tempCal.get(Calendar.Year);

// Time works the same way:
int hours = tempCal.get(Calendar.HOUR_OF_DAY);
int minutes = tempCal.get(Calendar.MINUTE);
int second = tempCal.get(Calendar.SECOND);

// If you want to increment a date element, like say, the day of month, you could
// use Calendar's "add" method, which accepts two integers: the first indicates which
// field within the Calendar's Date you want to increment, and the second indicates
// how many whole intervals you want to update it by (the number of intervals can be
// negative, which results in your decrementing the field instead of incrementing it).
// The following fields are available to you for manipulation:
// Calendar.MONTH
// Calendar.DAY_OF_MONTH
// Calendar.YEAR
// Calendar.HOUR_OF_DAY
// Calendar.MINUTE
// Calendar.SECOND
// EXAMPLE: Assuming we have a Date object called tempDate:
Calendar tempCal = Calendar.getInstance();
tempCal.setTime(tempDate);
// To increment the day of month by one day, use a positive value:
tempCal.add(Calendar.DAY_OF_MONTH, 1);
// If you want to decrement it by two instead, use a negative value:
tempCal.add(Calendar.DAY_OF_MONTH, -2);
// DateFormat is used to format dates for display.  I haven't used it much so far;
// I've generally always built my own Strings by hand, mostly because I'm
// obstinate, not because that's a good idea.  Here are some ways you can
// use DateFormat:

// Start out by creating a DateFormat object.  The best way to do this is to pass in
// the DateFormat constant that corresponds to the style of date you want to display
// Here are the formats you'll probably want to use:

// The SHORT format looks like "7/7/08".
DateFormat currentFormat = DateFormat.getDateInstance(DateFormat.SHORT);

// The MEDIUM format looks like "Jul 7, 2008".
DateFormat currentFormat = DateFormat.getDateInstance(DateFormat.MEDIUM);

// The LONG format looks like "July 7, 2008".
DateFormat currentFormat = DateFormat.getDateInstance(DateFormat.LONG);

// The FULL format looks like "Monday, July 7, 2008".
DateFormat currentFormat = DateFormat.getDateInstance(DateFormat.FULL);

// If you want to display time also, try using getDateTimeInstance() instead. Note
// that you can mix and match the style for the date and time formats. In the following,
// the first parameter is the date format and the second is the time format:

// The SHORT format looks like "7/7/08 4:29 PM".
```

DateFormat currentFormat = DateFormat.getDateTimeInstance(DateFormat.SHORT, DateFormat.SHORT);

// The MEDIUM format looks like "Jul 7, 2008 4:29:38 PM".
DateFormat currentFormat = DateFormat.getDateTimeInstance(DateFormat.MEDIUM, DateFormat.MEDIUM);

// The LONG format looks like "July 7, 2008 4:29:38 PM EDT".
DateFormat currentFormat = DateFormat.getDateTimeInstance(DateFormat.LONG, DateFormat.LONG);

// The FULL format looks like "Monday, July 7, 2008 4:29:38 PM EDT".
DateFormat currentFormat = DateFormat.getDateTimeInstance(DateFormat.FULL, DateFormat.FULL);

// Now, you might have noticed by now that there's no DateFormat that just produces
// "MM/DD/YYYY". I suppose you could try to set a NumberFormat, and write a bunch
// of irritating code to support that, but if you want to keep things simple, try this:

Calendar tempCal = Calendar.getInstance();
String monthString = Integer.toString(tempCal.get(Calendar.MONTH));
String dayString = Integer.toString(tempCal.get(Calendar.DAY_OF_MONTH));
String yearString = Integer.toString(tempCal.get(Calendar.YEAR));
if(monthString.length() < 2) monthString = "0" + month;
if(dayString.length() < 2) dayString = "0" + day;
String normalDate = monthString + "/" + dayString + "/" + yearString;

// It's not perfect, but it gives you the exact String you're looking for.

So that's enough to get you started with the Java Date object.

Afterword: Final Advice, Next Steps, Etc.

At this point, you should be somewhat comfortable with Java as a language, and you should be relatively confident that you can write actual, useful code. But so far you haven't built any real projects yet. Let's spend a last few minutes talking about where you should go from here.

The VERY FIRST thing you should do is run NetBeans and work your way through some of their excellent online documentation. There are some tutorials about how to build GUIs and applications right on their welcome page. This is the most logical starting point for you. Then, as soon as you have a basic idea of how to work with the IDE, start building little toy projects. One of my favorite "starter" projects is a "file viewer". This is a program that allows the user to select a file, then displays it in a scrolling window, usually supplying line numbers along the left hand side of the screen. There's enough information in this book and the NetBeans tutorials to get you going on this, and you'll learn a lot about building and testing applications through it. It shouldn't take more than a couple of days.

A great little book you can get right now in bookstores, which contains an amazingly useful set of recipes, is the "**Java Phrasebook**" by **Timothy R. Fisher**. It's very small, purple and white, and costs less than twenty bucks, but it contains tips on how to do EVERYTHING. I keep a copy in my courier bag when I go to work, it's wonderful. Wanna know how to generate emails from Java? Parse XML? It's all in there, in clear, concise instructions. Beautiful stuff, it's a must buy.

Once you're happily tinkering away on a few small projects, you'll find yourself getting used to Java very quickly. The next thing you should do is learn **iText**, the package I mentioned in the file I/O chapter. You can find this at http://www.lowagie.com/iText/, and believe me, you'll get a lot of use out of it. Every boss, sooner or later, wants you to generate PDFs. You can be ahead of the curve by learning it in advance. Here's a juicy tip I've learned from my work: You can create a PDF template, open it as an object, and populate the fields at runtime -- you don't have to generate everything by hand. This was a huge timesaver.

You can find all of my Java notes (everything I didn't put in the book) at my website. The Java section contains all the notes I've collected on how to do various things you might find useful, and the Technology section has tips and tricks for how to do various interesting sysop-type stuff. I'm going to add an Android section one of these days. You can find the website here: http://tech-hermitage.com/Java.

There's been a big push lately to dumb the language down, with people trying to use JavaFX and XML to build desktop applications. Their big excuse is "Swing is too hard". What nonsense. Swing is still the easiest and best way to develop for the desktop, and we shouldn't abandon it. It's not any more difficult than using DreamWeaver to build a web page; modern IDEs usually come with high quality graphical user interface designers (you can even get one for Eclipse now, although it's an extra download). In general, anyone who tells you "Swing is too hard" is trying to sell you something.

Don't let anyone tell you Java is only for web development. It's outstanding for web development, don't get me wrong. It's very powerful. But saying it's only good for web development is like saying cars are only good for commuting. There's a lot more to life than your commute. You drive to the store, to the cinema, to the city when you want to visit a nightclub, and to visit your family or go to the shore, don't you? Don't limit yourself.

Having said that, web development is a fairly dependable money maker for a Java programmer, so you'll want to learn how to write servlets and jsps relatively soon. If you're interested in this, I suggest you browse the O'Reilly catalog. They have some excellent books on the subject.

Here's something important: get into Android as fast as you can. Android uses (mostly) Java syntax, with the primary difference being that it has a different standard library. Having read this book, you already know Java syntax, so you can step right into Android. I highly recommend this... What Google has given us is a straightforward way to go independent. Whether you write your own apps or you freelance and sell apps to companies, don't overlook this opportunity. I'm certainly going to take advantage of it. If you hit it just right, you could make some serious cash. It is definitely possible.

I think Android development is similar to writing a novel in some ways. Sometimes writers barely make enough to get by, sometimes they make a reasonable living, and sometimes, they get ridiculously wealthy. Right? But all they have to do is write. It costs them nothing but their free time, a typewriter, and some paper. Even if they only make enough to get by, they've created something from nothing, and they've been paid for it. Android development is exactly the same. You have almost no up-front costs except for your free time, and you could potentially make a huge pile of cash. The only difference is that the Android Market is a lot easier to join than a publishing house.

Finally, I'd suggest that you consider Java to be something you'll be learning as long as you're working with it. There will always be some new trick or method to learn, you'll never run out of interesting or neat things to do with the language, and I think you probably are going to have a lot of fun playing with it. Good luck! And again, thanks for buying my book!